'In *Design & Grow*, Arte guide for designers to u ...ess concepts that will help th ...crease their efficiency, productivity and impact. Her clear and concise approach makes the complex concepts of business and economics accessible to even the most novice of designers, included a variety of tools and resources that will help designers to leverage their creative energy and become more successful in the workplace.'

> — **Allan Dib**, serial entrepreneur, rebellious marketer, #1 bestselling author

'A terrific and engaging read. Artemis sets easy-to-implement takeaways to help designers grow their businesses and tackle fundamental business issues. If you want practical tools and results, read this book.'

> — **Daniel Priestley**, award-winning author and entrepreneur

'Artemis sets out her secrets of how to become a successful designer in a clear and down-to-earth way, with practical examples that show the depth and breadth of her experience. Her STORMS method is easy to follow, and the reader can easily dive into each chapter as a standalone or take it as a whole. This book is a must-read for designers who are struggling with the business side of their design business.'

— **David B Horne**, award-winning author and entrepreneur

Design
& Grow

The six-step method to reach your
creative business potential, grow profits
and get your design time back

ARTEMIS DOUPA

Re think

First published in Great Britain in 2023
by Rethink Press (www.rethinkpress.com)

*To my family. My parents and brother,
and my beautiful husband and children.
You have all given me something special.
Being successful for me is to be able to do
what I love and still have time with all of you.*

Contents

Foreword

*D*esign & Grow is essential for all creators wanting to grow their businesses. The design world is a fascinating, fast paced and rewarding place to be, but it can be challenging, lonely, overwhelming and painful at times. Artemis' words, along with her detailed STORMS Method, will help you navigate the business world confidently, enlightening you whether a seasoned professional or just starting out.

With a front-row seat, I've witnessed Artemis and her partner Alexander navigate and grow their own successful businesses, working with renowned designers, celebrities, start-up companies and independent artists. They are incredibly experienced and always at the forefront of technology changes and advances. They cleverly and positively weave growth seamlessly into their business, and help many other people shape their own businesses for the better.

Design & Grow is a guide you'll want to revisit time and again, using the tasks to keep you on track as your business grows and changes. As a business owner myself, I love the fact that the balance of personal and work life is highlighted. In this industry, and many others, we often wear the busy badge of honour, but we can work smart and just as efficiently without always having to burn the midnight oil. This is something I've learnt the hard way. The systems Artemis puts in place within her book will effectively reinforce this, so you can dream big, aim high and grow a sustainable business whilst still enjoying life.

Many creatives often feel ashamed to share their struggles and failures, I used to be one of them. This is why I adore the authenticity and honest approach in Artemis' words and appreciate the stories and anecdotes which I know many creatives will find relatable. As I like to say, you deserve to go after your dreams just as much as anyone else, and Artemis has given the tools to do just that.

Rachael Taylor,
Co-founder of Make it in Design,
author and award-winning creative

Introduction

Design is in your blood, or so people say. If you are talented and passionate, you have more to offer than just creative work, but even if you are an entrepreneur at heart, starting and growing a business can be daunting, especially when your training was in something other than business.

This book is aimed at owners of established design businesses employing between three and twelve people. It's a step-by-step guide to claiming back your time – and making money – based on my own journey as a designer, architect, creative and mother who couldn't bear to give up any of it.

I have watched owners of small and not-so-small businesses face the same issues. They started because they love what they do, and then others loved it too and one thing led to another, and their business was born. Now they are stuck in an office under a pile of paperwork and responsibilities that have nothing to do with their love. No design, no big picture, no time and no money.

Imagine growing your business profitably with a team that thrives while you're flying off to the Caribbean. Wait a minute – did I say you'd need to take your laptop? You can leave that at home and focus on your holiday with your loved ones. If that sounds attractive to you, then you and I have work to do.

After many years as chief executive officer (CEO) of maake, a bespoke fabric printing business that I co-founded with the highly talented Alexander Wills, I have learned that creative business own-ers face a world of pain – because I was there once myself, but also because I constantly come across individuals who are offering great products and great vision that the market would be lucky to have, but who are invisible. They lack the business skills to cope as the company demands grow, and then the cracks appear – first financial cracks, then team issues, and often quality issues. This can have a big impact on confidence and spiral into a loop of uncer-tainty and confusion.

If this is you, I know your pain.

I decided that enough is enough. In 2019, I started a new business venture, now maakeAcademy, and opened my doors to those who want to make their mark in the design industry – successfully.

Trapped in your dream?

People say I have a photographic memory, and it does help me to connect people, places, designs and other details I have come across to come up with solutions. Why am I telling you this? Because maakeAcademy started in exactly this way: watching fabric come off the press in the maake factory and connecting with one of our designers.

Watching fabric print calms me. It also inspires me. All those beautiful designs and colours mapped strategically to create a pattern, a vision. No wonder fabric rolls spinning make for attention-grabbing social-media posts – it's mesmerising. Ellie (not her real name), a talented designer, used to print with us consistently for two years, but suddenly, she stopped. When I realised that I no longer saw her patterns appearing on our fabrics, I decided to give her a call.

'I haven't seen your work in a while,' I said. 'Are you working on anything new?'

She was quiet for a few moments, then said, her voice trembling, 'I just can't do it anymore. I am trapped in my dream. No matter what I do, I don't seem to make headway. I am a designer, not an entrepreneur.'

That got to me. Why can't you be both?

We spoke for a while and Ellie explained that things weren't going well at all. She had no time to design because she was buried under endless paper-work. Running her team was harder than disciplining her three kids, who she never got to spend any quality time with anymore. She wasn't sure where to go from here.

Ellie has a background in fashion and pattern making. Her work was featured in *Vogue* and her business grew quickly as a result. What didn't grow was her business knowledge. She was lacking effective marketing, sales and operational systems, and as a result, she was running out of money and time to focus on what she loved.

I felt for her. I know what it is like to learn about business the hard way and I didn't want to see a talented designer fail when I knew she could fix it. We met shortly after that call and made a plan – which changed both our lives.

Not long afterwards, while I was watching our fabric printers, I noticed a pattern. It made me smile; it was Ellie's. She was printing again. Later that week, I got a call from her.

'Hey, I am getting the hang of it. All the work we have done together is taking shape. My systems are working, and my marketing is blooming. I've even planned a holiday with my family.'

Ellie did it, and so can you.

Thanks to the work I did with Ellie, as well as many entrepreneurs after her, I have recognised the most common mistakes made by creative business owners and understand which changes give a true tilt to the scale. Through helping them to get it right, I developed my STORMS method, and maakeAcademy was born.

The STORMS method

Like a recipe for your favourite meal, a successful business requires certain ingredients in certain measures: a bit too much or too little of something, and the whole dish can disappoint. This doesn't mean that it's inedible (well, not always); it means it's hard to swallow. Even though you've had your dinner, you don't feel satisfied.

Business can be a little like that. You start all excited and invest in the best ingredients – a beautiful workspace, quality materials, a fancy laptop – and suddenly things get real. You and your team throw yourselves into marketing. Orders come in, and you take them all on so you can survive the month.

You make more and more sales, and you become overwhelmed. Perhaps you didn't expect your marketing campaign to go quite so well, and now you wonder how you will fulfil all these orders. Your team is lining up with questions, and the phone is ringing constantly – orders, queries, complaints and, to top it all, the school calls to say you need to pick your child up as they're sick.

I want you to know, there *is* a way out of this increasing financial and workload pressure and its negative impact on your personal life and wellbeing.

I've seen what works and what doesn't while working with many companies, both large and small (I can't name drop – big brands have NDAs – but if you go to fashion shows, watch Netflix or shop at either the High Street or Harrods, you've likely seen our work). I've observed and identified six crucial elements that ensure everything remains well oiled, and these elements make up the STORMS method.

You may have come across some or all of these elements before, but how do you know if they are all equally important, which one to start with, and what happens if you don't consider or implement all of them?

In fact, *every* element of your organisation, however small, plays a key role in your business and your personal success (as they say at my son's kickboxing classes, 'You might be small, but you are a mighty force'). Individually and together, these elements are extremely powerful.

The STORMS method provides clarity and focus on what matters and stops you spending time and resources in the wrong area. Ultimately, working hard doesn't necessarily make you stand out – but working smart does.

Let's have a look at the elements of the STORMS method:

- Systems

- Team

- Operations

- Reaction

- Marketing

- Sustainability

Systems – your brand's personality

If everyone expects to get their answers from you, then you are the system. You are essential to your business, and that is a dangerous thing. If there is nothing on paper because it is all in your head, and you want to exit your business at some point, this lack of systems may put off potential buyers and can hugely impact the scale of any offer you may get. Implement effective and transparent systems and your life, and your company, will be transformed.

Team – together we can move mountains

A company is only as strong as its team. Know how to pick the right people, and your team will thrive. It's the process you use to recruit – not the highest salaries – that will allow you to achieve an extraordinary vision with ordinary people.

Operations – stop being an octopus

Running your own business is exhilarating and exhausting in equal measures. If you feel that you have to oversee every department, you may end up needing more arms than an octopus to keep on top of things. If accounting, sales and other operational tasks seem daunting, find someone who loves and is as good at this work as you are at the creative and design process.

Reaction – your mind will lead you to greatness

Your mindset is going to determine if your brand will make it to the big league or not. Mindset is not a magical key to success, but it can help you control your reaction to, and act on, what goes on around you to get results. Know who you are inside and, more importantly, who you believe you can be, and get out what you invest: you have the power.

Marketing – observe, act, iterate

Designers are no strangers to testing colours, compositions, patterns and so much more. In the same way, marketing needs a bit of testing, and data you can get from the multitude of today's marketing channels and tested techniques can give your brand an edge – no more shots in the dark.

Sustainability – 'I used to be a plastic bottle,' said the dress

I don't think I even need to say how important our actions as designers are to the environment and our children's future. We all play a part and should take small, inexpensive steps to ensure we do better for our business and our planet.

Make your mark

You are unique and talented. You have what it takes, otherwise you wouldn't have made it this far. Enabling you to do what you love is the number one priority of this book. Having fun as an entrepreneur is what can tip the scales from enduring a daily business nightmare, no matter the profit, to enjoying business success.

The STORMS method will enable you to get back your creative focus *and* grow your business. To get the most out of it, I strongly recommend that you follow it in the order that it has been designed.

If you take on board its well-crafted knowledge, follow the tried-and-tested techniques and carry out the actionable tasks in each chapter, this book can help you build a successful business that will allow your creativity to flourish, make you money, and then some more.

1
Systems

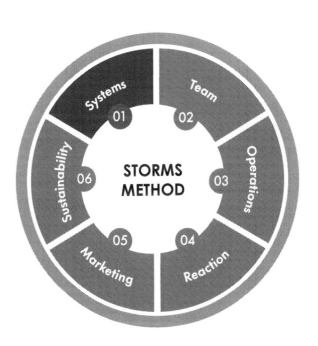

CHAPTER SUMMARY

The S in STORMS stands for systems. Systems are assets you can't ignore: a lack of effective systems cause bottlenecks that every business owner needs to tackle as soon as possible.

This chapter covers:

- What a system is, and why it is so important
- The Four Ds – design, decide, delegate, document
- How to document your systems efficiently
- Why people don't follow systems and what to do about it

1
Systems

Running a business that relies on your knowledge and ability to answer questions every minute of the day is exhausting. The fun goes out of the window and you end up staring at the computer screen thinking, 'Where did my day go?'.

At every meeting there is a moment of truth and clarity. The following case study explains what I mean.

CASE STUDY: Have you seen my new collection? It's the same as the old one

I remember the day I arrived for a scheduled meeting with a business owner – let's call her Helen – and rang the bell of her premises. There was no answer. I tried again and finally someone opened the door.

'Can I help you?' a man asked. I explained I was there to see Helen for our appointment at eleven o'clock. 'Oh, right, right,' he said and let me in. Then he rushed off and disappeared.

I walked in what I assumed was the right direction. As I kept walking, the man rushed back to show me the way to Helen's office. I was amused. Even though the place appeared organised and clean, here was a company of ten people, none of whom had any idea how to receive guests to their offices. They clearly had no systems in place.

Helen was as delightful as she was talented. She started by explaining to me how she had always loved designing clothes, and when her brother became a father, she made baby clothes for the new arrival. Everyone in the family loved the fabrics and the stories she told of the inspiration behind her designs, which encouraged her to start selling in the marketplace.

'I started in my own kitchen six years ago,' Helen said, 'and look at me now – I can afford an office.' Proud and passionate though she was about what she was doing, the excitement faded from her eyes as she finished her story.

'I am tired,' she said. 'I haven't been on holiday in forever. I barely see my kids anymore and my husband is fed up with me refusing to take any time off.'

She explained that a few years ago, she went on a two-week holiday and ended up on the phone for the entire trip. Orders went out wrong, customers were upset, and she was so stressed that all she wanted was to take a flight back.

As she was talking, the door opened. A young woman entered.

'Excuse me,' she said. 'I don't mean to interrupt, but I have a question.' Helen spent at least five minutes answering her team member's question. Then the team member apologised once more and left, and we continued our chat.

'Have you seen my new collection?' Helen asked me. Before I could even respond, she continued, 'Actually, it's much the same as the old collection. I took those designs and changed them up a bit. There is no time for me to design anymore.'

Then another employee showed up with another question. Less than an hour had passed and already two employees had interrupted our meeting. I looked at Helen and asked her if this was something that happened a lot.

'Yes, this happens all day long,' she said with a sigh. 'People come in and out in a constant stream, asking questions.'

I had stayed long enough to realise that Helen had problems in her business, and her number-one problem was that she had no systems. She lacked consistency and wasn't training her staff in an effective way, so her company depended entirely on her. Employees didn't make the effort to learn or take ownership because they knew that she was just a phone call away or physically at the office. She had to answer queries all day to help production and design as well as cover her own workload. Even if she was in a meeting, employees felt that they could disturb her instead of figuring out a solution to the problem themselves. Without her input, things ran the risk of falling apart.

Does Helen's story sound familiar to you? You are not alone.

You can't be the business

If you feel overwhelmed like Helen – and who doesn't at some point in business? – it's essential that you face the issue. A lot of design businesses are built by talented people with no time to do what they love because their employees are relying on them too much.

If you want to have a successful business, you can't *be* the business. You read that right. If you are at the core of your business, that is a recipe for endless trouble. Allowing yourself to step back is surprisingly good for your business, because only then do you truly see what you have achieved.

If your business has experienced rapid growth like Helen's, it is easy to skip steps and rush into hiring to grow the business further. You feel invincible because sales are coming in and everything seems like it will work out. You feel like you've finally made it.

When a problem arises and an issue surfaces, you and your team get confused. Whose fault is it? No one on the team is sure exactly what they are meant to be doing. You all used to do two or three jobs when there were only five of you, but now there are ten, you end up putting out daily fires instead of concentrating on improving your business or your product.

Whose role is it?

In my household, we have a traditional approach to tasks. My husband knows he has to deal with the tax return as well as any car-related issues. I know I order the food and cook, make sure the house is tidy and get the kids to their activities on time. This arrangement has settled in over the years, a sort of unspoken role allocation. I asked my husband a couple of times to do my tax and deal with the car, and since then I've never had to ask about or do those tasks again.

For better or worse, we have trained each other to do 'our' tasks and just not get involved in those that we don't perceive to be our responsibility anymore. If I explained what's on the list for our weekly food shop and asked him to do the shopping twice a month, he probably would. If he explained to me how to deal with my car issues, I probably would. But we both just deal with these things ourselves, because it's easier than having to explain it to the other or taking the trouble to learn.

Having said that, creating accountability and laying down expectations right from the beginning is essential in business (as well as in life). It is human nature to fall into old habits, but you do not want your employees to take a back seat. You need them to be self-starters and problem solvers within your company.

For this to happen, you need to be clear on your rules. No employee should ever interrupt a meeting.

No client should ever be received by an employee who has no idea they are coming. You let it happen once and it becomes a habit.

CASE STUDY: My company is doing great

A friend I hadn't seen in a long time sat down with me for a coffee one day. Max (not his real name) got straight to the point.

'I don't know how to handle this. Can you help?' he asked.

I could tell he was really anxious. He had finally been asked to take over the family business from his father. He'd known this was coming and was very excited, but after speaking to his parents and some of the employees, he'd started to panic.

His father wanted him to oversee the business and have a say on everything from finance and human resources (HR) to public relations, marketing strategies and so on. This in a business that may have started from zero, but after thirty years was comfortably trading at an eight-figure level. It was going strong.

I asked Max how the company's systems were documented and implemented.

'We have no systems,' he said. 'The employees have learnt the job from each other over the years and we have kept them on for decades, creating a family environment. Hardly anyone has been fired, even when they should be, and no one follows a system apart from their own.'

I wasn't shocked; this was not the first time I'd heard of a situation like this. It's far more common than you may think.

Experience and routine were this company's systems. The problem was that Max's father and mother had overseen everything as they wanted to keep control. His father would even spend half of his workday researching alternatives for a new professional vacuum cleaner because he was so determined to keep costs to a minimum, ignoring all the money pouring out from lack of efficiency across the departments. For a company with 100–150 employees, this approach was madness.

'You are in quite the situation,' I said. 'How soon are you taking over? We can fix this.' What was important was that Max knew things had to change. He realised that without his parents, there was no more family business. Without them, there was no business at all. No matter how great his ideas were or how experienced he was in his field. The company needed systems – there was no question about that.

Over the years, I have come across many small and medium business owners who haven't understood the benefits of systems. They ignore them for years and only when they seek help do they realise all the opportunities they have missed out on: an important interview; a trip abroad; conferences; speaking invitations; even having children.

Best-case scenario: you are invited to your dream interview, a fashion show or interior-design show abroad, or your idol designer or entrepreneur asks you to shadow them for three months. Worst case scenario: you have an accident and are stuck in bed for a while. Either way, a lack of systems will hold both you and the business back. By sacrificing your precious time by answering questions from employees, you're restricting improvements and failing to identify weak links in your departments.

You can't overcome obstacles when you struggle to identify them. To improve performance and achieve extraordinary results, you need to equip yourself and your team with reliable systems. Systems will allow your business to achieve sustainable growth and become scalable, and something a lot of entrepreneurs miss is that systems also make your company saleable. Not everyone wants to sell one day, but why not have the option? There is no harm in being ready.

If you ever want or have to sell, the value of your company will be determined by its assets. No one will pay you big money unless your company has measurable assets and top of the list will be your systems.

What is a system?

A system is a series of instructions; a guide of how to do something. It can be something as simple as how you make your coffee, or even how you like your pasta. I doubt many people have a system for that, but I do:

1. Setting up is essential to me. I make sure my phone is to hand so I can have an accurate timer; I don't use the timer in the kitchen as I want to be exact.

2. Using the thin grater, I grate some cheese while the pasta is boiling. I place some of the cheese on the

bottom of my plate – even though Italians I know get completely furious with me for doing that – and the rest I keep on the side for later.

3. I take the pasta out at the exact time, depending on the brand – some needs thirty seconds more – and put a layer on the plate.

4. Add more cheese.

5. Add more pasta.

6. Then add the sauce on the side of the plate.

7. Add a piece of feta, keeping it separate from the sauce and the pasta (I don't want it to get warm).

8. Ready.

I know what you might be thinking – but that's me. Why not put the cheese on top like most people and mix the pasta? Because I have found early on that when I mix the pasta and the cheese, it cools the pasta down far too quickly. That makes me lose the joy of my meal as I love my food hot.

Everyone does things their own way at home and in business. We alter a basic action to suit ourselves, our customers, our industry and so on. Would you succeed in preparing pasta exactly to my liking after reading my system? Are you thinking of course you would? If so, you may be surprised to hear that my mother always gets my pasta wrong, even though she is the most loving mother and wants to please me no end. On the other hand, my husband, who I have known way less time than my mother, (almost) always gets it right.

Why is it so hard to get employees to follow simple instructions? Because it's human nature – everyone has their own way of doing things. Sometimes, they think they can improve on your system and make it better (like my mother). Others are too arrogant or too forgetful or even too stressed and overworked to follow everything you say and return a perfect result.

Standard operation procedures (SOPs) were created for one reason: to make sure that everyone in the team is on the same page. When you get a recipe, you know that if you follow it exactly, you will have a decent meal. You know if you practise, you will improve and make cooking the meal easier, and it will be consistently good. If you start altering it to your taste or inspiration (i.e. optimise it) after you master it, you could arrive at an even better result. On the other hand, if you read out the recipe to someone once and expect them to produce the same result, you will most likely end up hungry and disappointed.

Processes, procedures or systems: they go by many names, but at their core is a series of simple steps that you and your employees follow to get a *predictable outcome* with no fail. We all use systems in our daily lives and our businesses, even if we are not aware of them.

Whether it's the system you use to hire new staff or the way your employees request stock, do not underestimate the importance of consistency. Your customers expect the same steps, service and quality every time. Imagine going to your favourite restaurant where the service is usually next to perfection, but this time it is poor. This would likely leave you with a negative emotional connection to the experience that will prevent you from rushing back. No matter how connected you are to a brand, one bad experience can be all it takes to put you off.

Make changes smooth

People in general don't love change, even positive change. You may have spent a small fortune on a new uplift for your website and be super excited, but suddenly find your customers are getting frustrated and sales are decreasing as a result. It's the same with systems. Any change in your company's systems needs to be introduced smoothly and strategically. I am in no way suggesting you shouldn't strive for positive changes; I am simply pointing out that all your stakeholders – both customers and employees – need smooth transitions.

Ultimately, all business deficiencies can be traced back to a lack of decent systems. Poor marketing strategy or data collection can lead to overspend on adverts and no or low-quality leads. A recruitment system that is lacking can lead to unsuitable employees and affect the company culture, increasing turnover. A poor financial system can cause serious cash-flow issues.

All your systems are connected; you can't work on one without thinking of the others. The business is like a living organism: it needs to be healthy in all aspects. You can't survive if one of your organs is malfunctioning – sooner or later, it will become a whole-body problem. It is the same for your business. Each department plays a role and they all deserve the same amount of attention to complement each other.

The Four Ds

When people think of systems, they often imagine endless folders collecting dust on a shelf or tucked at the back of a drawer. Outdated manuals that no one ever reads. That doesn't sound particularly motivating, but this is not the path you are going to take. You can create systems that are easy to access, short and comprehensive. Sound better? I hope so, because I need you on board with this.

If you are someone who can't afford to run out of battery life on your phone otherwise it is likely to spell disaster for your business and a holiday seems like a distant dream, then know that I was in your shoes for years when I started my first business. I now realise that if you are in this position, you are there for one reason only: your systems are not doing their job. You may have too many or too few or the wrong ones, or maybe you never had the time to get around to creating them and you have none.

Here's the good news. In fact, it's great news: this is the moment everything will fall into place. I've worked with hundreds of business owners in the fashion and interior-design industry over the years and have devised an easy way for them – and you – to create systems to get their businesses in order. I call it the Four Ds:

- Design
- Decide
- Delegate
- Document

How long will it take to implement? That depends on how big and complex your business is. It might take you three to twelve months with a bit of help, or if you decide to do it yourself, it is likely to take a lot longer. One thing is for sure, it will be worth it in the end.

The next bit of good news is that you don't have to do it alone; you have a team and they will need to take an active part in this process. Did I miss out the best part? Most systems are not meant to be written by the founders. Did your day get a little brighter on hearing that? Yes, that's right: overall, you are not going to be writing your company's systems. Your team is.

Design

Start with design. Designing your business systems can give you clarity in many areas and identify what steps you are missing or need to improve. The key is to keep things simple.

The core of your business is your customer journey, so that's what you focus on. You and your team may have many ideas on new ways to improve the journey, but I urge you to write down only what you are currently doing. There will be time for optimising later.

To help with this step, you can head to www.maakeacademy.com/designandgrow and download the pdf for your customer journey. You will find a template to fill in and two examples.

There are six main steps on the customer journey. Be open minded and don't rush into the common thinking that your business is different, so these steps don't apply. Yes, you have your unique selling points, but all businesses are the same at the core. I have faith that you will make this model work.

Step 1: Capture

This refers to the different ways you capture a prospective customer's attention and data. How do people contact you? Can they find your number easily? Do you have it on banners, catalogues, cards, your website, etc?

There are several ways for prospects to contact you nowadays and this step is about identifying these ways. Is it by phone, email or contact form? If you are local, you might even have people showing up at your factory or shop.

From the moment a customer has contacted you, they can be divided into two categories: ready to buy and leads (which can be further divided into warm/

cold leads). The journey for these two types of custom-ers is different and it's crucial to understand which category each customer falls into. We will explore this a lot further in the 'Marketing' chapter, but for now, we'll follow the full journey for a customer who is ready to buy.

Step 2: Sales

You are now visible to your customer. Pat yourself on the back as this is good news. Ready-to-buy cus-tomers take direct action to contact you with specific questions and start your sales journey.

Depending on how a customer contacts you initially, you generally respond through the same channel. Each channel will collect some details, but ultimately, the sales process will lead to a discovery call where the customer will go over the worries or needs they have (their pain points). You then pre-pare a proposal and a quote, if you can offer a viable solution or direct them to your website. Finally, you prepare an invoice and organise a payment transac-tion with the customer.

Step 3: Production

This is the fun part where your team needs to be tuned in and ready to deliver a quality product. Depending on your brand, this may involve an artwork studio, sourcing, cutting, sewing, folding or any other kind of producing. Identify your production areas and group them depending on your teams of employees.

Step 4: Delivery

Making the delivery of your product a world-class experience deserves its own step. You could deliver it in person, by mail, digitally or by customer collection. In each of these instances, make the experience as wonderful and painless as possible.

Step 5: After sales

You have made a sale, but this is not the end of the journey. There may be returns (depending on your business's services) due to faults or unhappy customers. There may be issues with the delivery or the product itself. Hopefully, in most cases, the sale will be successful, and you will receive a shining review from the customer.

Step 6: Follow up

This final step on the customer journey is often left out, but it is crucial to your business. After the sale, nurture the client and work towards a repeat order. If you don't have this step in your business yet, there is no need to worry as we will be covering it in the 'Marketing' chapter.

The customer journey worksheet

It's time to fill up the customer journey worksheet. In order to keep the design of your systems simple, start by identifying the main areas of the journey your customer takes. The content of each step will help you create your fundamental systems. When you identify the steps your different departments take to complete their tasks, you will be able to refer back to your customer journey template and prioritise the completion of the systems that will make the biggest impact in your team.

Decide

Your job as an entrepreneur is to solve problems, whether it be in the market or in your business. The most successful entrepreneurs are not necessarily those who finish business school and have Master of Business Administration degrees. Although this qualification is helpful, it is not essential. True entrepreneurs have a gift, naturally or thanks to the way they were raised, to solve problems. They identify the issue and their minds run towards finding the solution.

As you are still reading, I can tell you are a problem solver, and even though your business might need a bit of tweaking, you are not giving up. 'See the forest, not the trees,' my mother says, as many have done before her. Your brand's growth is linked to your vision. You will do what it takes to make your business successful, but you need to break free from the temptation to micromanage.

Step 1: Capture. How do people contact you? Phone, email, contact form, etc

> Speaking events | Facebook adverts | Phone | Website

Step 2: Sales. Discovery call (if appropriate), invoice, or website and payment transaction

> Phone | Discovery call | Proposal | Invoice

Step 3: Production. Artwork, sourcing, cutting, sewing, folding, etc

> Project set up | Making | Shipping

Step 4: Delivery. In person, by mail, pick up, etc

> By mail | In person

Step 5: After sale. Returns, complaints, delays

> Off-boarding call | Email

Step 6: Follow up. Nurture the customer. Work towards repeat orders.

> Add to database | Ongoing services

An example of a customer journey

Step by step, you can do it. All your teams are focusing on their own tasks, so it is essential to break down and clearly define those tasks. This will unfold the connections between the different departments/ employees, the issues they may have and the way they communicate.

The table coming up focuses on nine typical business departments and their tasks: organisation, marketing, sales, finance, operations, HR, strategy, management and customer service (CS). For example, marketing is responsible for search engine optimisation (SEO), email marketing, avatars (customer profile), segmentation of client lists, adverts, pay-per-click (PPC) and so on. The sales department is responsible for phone sales, discovery calls, follow ups and so on.

Visit www.maakeacademy.com/designandgrow to download the who-does-what (WDW) template and an example of how to fill it in.

Naturally, all these tasks have subcategories that they expand into, but for now, it is enough just to document each task/step in general terms.

A company can have many or few departments depending on its size and services. When you fill up your WDW sheet, you can add or remove departments to suit your brand; for example, you may include information technology (IT) and product development. In my business, I insist on having an organisation department which is visible to all employees and covers the basics that everyone needs to be aware of.

Organisation	Marketing	Sales
• Meetings • Templates • How to write SOPs • General essentials • Remote working	• Management • Avatars • Strategy • Branding • Copywriting	• Phone • Forms • In person • Client meetings • Training
Finance	**Operations**	**HR**
• Invoicing • Reports • Strategy • Projections	• Website • Factory • Artwork • Packing • Dispatch	• Holidays • Absences • Employee reports • Hiring • Firing
Strategy	**Management**	**Customer Service**
• Meetings • Reports • Speaking events • Vision • Pitch	• Meetings • Reports/KPIs • Training • Optimising • Team morale	• Canned responses • Back end/ website • Phones • CS software • Training

Example of an initial who-does-what (WDW) sheet

When you have filled in your WDW sheet, compare it with your customer journey and highlight the most important actions in each department. This will help you decide which systems to prioritise. Use a different colour highlighter for the most problematic areas – those that are causing the customer the biggest frustration. Another way to prioritise is to select the areas where each team makes the most mistakes or is the most inconsistent.

Branding plays a big role in your marketing and the way you view your business, so reflect this in your SOP systems. Before you start making any decisions concerning your systems, get your team to create a template with the fonts and colours that are representative of your branding. This will create the impression that your company takes its systems seriously. Decide on a template and how you expect your files to be named.

Your 'systems' document needs to be something you can proudly show to your employees, recruits and future investors or buyers. Think of it as a system for your systems.

Where will the systems be stored? If you run a company of fewer than twenty people, I wouldn't bother with SOP software. Any work management software would be more than sufficient, Monday. com, Trello and Asana being among the most popular ones. As the world of software and technology moves so fast, you can visit www.maakeacademy. com/designandgrow for updated information and suggestions.

When you've decided on the software in which you want your systems to live, you can add more information (depending on the functions of the software) such as links, files, people and reminders. This can be helpful at a later stage for optimising and perfecting your systems. It is also a great way to allocate tasks quickly and leave notes about training or revision sessions.

You should also be able to allow or restrict access to team members, depending on the department they work in. Not everyone needs to know everything. In fact, you most certainly want to restrict access to certain departments or documents. Your systems are part of your company's intellectual property, so it is vital you use them to improve your services without overwhelming or confusing your staff members. Allow your team members access to the systems they need to perform their job to the highest standard.

Delegate

The *Oxford Dictionary of English* defines the verb 'delegate' as '…entrust (a task or responsibility) to another person, typically one who is less senior than oneself'.[1]

The key word here is *entrust*. You need to entrust your employees and create a culture where they will be confident and motivated to take ownership of a task. Each person will be fully accountable to complete the task to the best of their ability.

Delegation is a core value in business that allows the founder and leaders to run a smooth operation. The better you and your leadership team are at delegating, the more you can reduce secondary tasks and free up time for yourself to focus on growing your business. This will allow you to put your time into the vital few areas which will tip the scale for your business growth.

It is a myth that all a company's systems should be created by the owner. You need to follow your instinct as well as logic. When your company is small (five to ten people), you already have systems that your staff are using daily, even if they aren't documented. Instead of starting from nothing, delegate the task to be systemised to your team members. Get each one to write down how they complete their daily tasks as they do them. Then you review their systems and edit them to your preferences.

The benefit of having your team members compile the systems is that they will be more likely to follow them. It gets them involved in the change to the company becoming more systematised, but it is vital that the systems reflect how you expect the tasks to be done. There will, of course, be systems that only you as the business owner can document, including those for working with external partners, possibly accounting, HR and, most importantly, strategic documents and confidential systems.

Now it's time to get specific. If you haven't already downloaded the WDW document, visit www.maakeacademy.com/designandgrow. On your WDW sheet, you have identified what each department covers, it's time to decide which member of the team will do each task.

In the person column, as shown in the example below, write the name of the team member who will be responsible for delivering each system. If your team is small, you might find the same names coming up again and again, and that's absolutely fine.

Organisation		Marketing		Sales	
Meetings	Mary	Management	Mary	Phone	John
Templates	John	Avatars	Helen	Forms	Helen
How to write SOPs	Mary	Strategy	Helen	In person	John
		Branding	Helen	Client meetings	John
General essentials	John	Copywriting	Mary		
Remote working	John			Training	John
Finance		**Operations**		**HR**	
Invoicing	Ben	Website	Kira	Holidays	Liam
Reports	Ben	Factory	Anna	Absences	Liam
Strategy	Ben	Artwork	Kira	Employee report	Liam
Projections	Alan	Packing	Anna	Hiring	Mary
		Dispatch	Anna	Firing	Mary
Strategy		**Management**		**Customer service**	
Meetings	Alan	Meetings	John	Canned responses	Jamie
Reports	Alan	Reports/KPIs	Kira	Back end/ website	Norma
Speaking events	Alan	Training	John		
		Optimising	Kira	Phones	Jamie
Vision	Alan	Team morale	Kira	CS software	Norma
Pitch	Alan			Training	Norma

Example of an advanced WDW diagram

Document

Now that you are clear on all your departments and who is doing what, it is time for the managers to expand on the tasks, actions and documents that are essential for their department. The easy way to explain this to your employees is to get them to imagine a comprehensive guide that anyone could pick up and use to complete a task when the person who normally covers that task is absent. Explain that no one wants to bother another staff member while they are on holiday, for example, just to ask how to do something. Your guide will ensure that every department will always be running smoothly and even improving.

Each of the tasks you have placed in your WDW sheet can be split into smaller subcategories, which should be included in the relevant systems document. Organising each department and clarifying what tasks it covers before anyone starts writing the systems will ensure that you eliminate both repetition and missing tasks, preventing you and your teams from becoming buried under endless mixed paperwork.

Think of your departments as a table of contents. With the CS department, for example, the subcategories would be canned responses, back end, phones, CS software, training. Each of those is a heading in its own right that can be split up into many more sections, covering as much or as little as your team needs.

In the table, you can see some simple examples of a breakdown of content for a CS systems document.

This is just the beginning; you can expand each section as required to reflect your company's complexity. For example:

1. **General**

   - Main management software boards and how to use them

   - Daily tasks

   - Company values and who we are

   - Spotting corrupt files

   - First response

   - Tone and voice

2. **Canned responses**

   - What are canned responses?

   - How and why to use them

   - Adding new responses process

3. **Back end/website**

   - Orders

   - Invoicing

   - Shipment

   - Credits

- Returns
- Issues with log in

4. **Training**
   - How to combine reports
   - Software essentials and tricks
   - How to use tags
   - Segmenting customers
   - Call trackers

A Word document using headings is more than sufficient for your documents to be organised and professional. Remember, though, that you and your team should be using a consistent template. Once your team gets familiar with the content, they can quickly link to the appropriate section of the document and find the systems they need without having to ask you or another member of the team.

You can add the content of your documents into your management system. This is a great way to keep notes and create clarity so your team will know what each document covers without even needing to open it, making this an effective way to organise your systems. Avoid at all costs printing out hundreds of pages and clipping them into folders. We are living in a digital world, so use a digital system to store your SOPs if you can.

There are different methods and media you can use to create your systems. Your staff members can simply take the list of tasks to be systemised that you delegate to them and allocate a set number of hours per week to documenting what they do daily on each task. Another way is to select an employee to be the SOP master who will create a schedule to partner up with each member of the team. The SOP master shadows each team member and documents all their tasks, asking questions when they're unclear on anything.

Your team can use voice-recording or video devices for reference when they're documenting the systems. These recordings can then be used for internal training. If you are more traditional, a pen and paper will do just as well. I strongly recommend that if you use voice recordings and video, you still document your systems with a contents page. It can be difficult for employees to find specific answers when they're going through video footage.

Once each task has been documented, the SOP master will be responsible for creating the written system for that task. They can then return to the team member to ensure the system is correctly documented. When it is approved, you as the director/founder can go over it with your leadership team and make notes on what doesn't work for you and ideas on how to improve it.

At the completion of your notes, call a meeting to discuss the changes with the person(s) who performs the tasks, what they will now be doing differently and how you expect the tasks to be done. This will allow you to understand your team member's point of view, and then come to a measured decision together on whether to accept or reject habits / techniques they have developed over the years. At the end of this process, the system for that particular task will be documented exactly as you and your team members want it. Two minds are better than one, so ten minds (if you have that many people on your team) will surely have a wealth of ideas. Respect your employees' opinions and allow them to express their point of view freely, even if you decide that your way is still the right one for your business.

Your first system

In his book *All of Grace,* nineteenth-century preacher Charles Spurgeon wrote 'Begin as you mean to go on',[2] and this is as relevant today as it was then. Start with the system that shows how to make systems. This will help your team understand why this process is so important. Talk to your team(s) at length; make them feel part of the journey and encourage them to strive for the common goal, which is the success of the business.

Who should make the system for making the systems? Depending on your team size, pick an organised, system-minded employee with an eye for design who will follow your brand guidelines confidently. You might have to be involved in this process a bit more than you will for the design of the subsequent systems as you want to ensure it reflects the company's standards.

What should the first system include? I have created a brief checklist of essentials, but you can add items as you see fit:

Checklist:

- Template – ensure you have a contents page which links to each section.

- How do you allocate new systems to staff members? Who allocates them?

- How long will each system take to create?

- How will you name your files?

- Where will the system be stored?

- What media will you use?

Once you know how you want the document to look and where it will be stored, consider the media you would like to record it with. You can use video as additional support to your text, diagrams and images. I avoid images unless they are evergreen as they can become outdated quite quickly. You can also use links to other documents if needed.

Now you are ready to create one of your most important assets.

Why is no one following your systems?

Your systems are all documented, and your work is done – or so you may think. This is a great start and you should be proud. Reward yourself for this achievement and take a big breath for what's coming.

When all your systems are beautifully organised into your files and you've overcome objections and taken on feedback from employees, you may well notice that even though your teams wrote them, they are not actually following them. Putting these systems together was so time consuming, but was it worth it?

The answer is a firm *yes*. This is the best thing you will have committed to doing in a while. Now let's get those unruly employees on board before you lose hope.

In the first chapter of his brilliant book *How To Win Friends and Influence People* (which is a must read if you want to improve your employee culture and overall social skills), self-help expert Dale Carnegie wrote 'By criticising, we do not make lasting changes and often incur resentment'.[3] He continued with a story of a safety coordinator who would walk around a construction site, using his authority to force the workers to wear their hard hats. The workers would put the hats on, but the moment he walked away, they would take them off again.

This became so frustrating, the safety coordinator decided to use a different approach. The next time he came across the workers without their hats on, he asked if the hats were uncomfortable or if there was any other issue with them. Then he went on to explain how they had been designed to protect the workers from injury, but only if they were worn at all times. The result was an increase in compliance and positive emotional response from the workers rather than resentment.

This is the kind of positive response to your systems that you are looking for from your employees. Start by speaking to your department manager(s) or the person in charge of each team. If you don't have a team hierarchy yet, pick the person you believe would make the best team leader. You need to motivate and encourage them to follow the systems, so explain again in a positive tone how important they are for both the company and employees. Benefits such as experiencing less stress, making fewer errors, having to put in less effort to get a job done, having more impact and fun as a team member, and even getting promoted are likely to follow. Focus on the benefits to the team and brainstorm ways to improve the culture. You are aiming to turn it into a system-oriented culture.

When you have your employees on board, ensure your whole team is familiar with the software you decide to use to store your systems and the way they are organised. Book in training days and set goals and expectations among your teams. When everyone is familiar with the systems and where to find them, they will be less likely to show resistance.

There will be those who won't follow the systems – you won't be able to get everyone on board. Some people are just too rebellious or arrogant or feel too entitled in their position after years of service, so they believe they are above any system change within the company. I'm sure you know what you need to do with these people. It is not easy and it might seem unfair to some, but the truth is that you can't make anyone do something unless they are willing. Not everyone belongs in your team, no matter how knowledgeable they are. We will explore employee values and qualities more in the next chapter, which will make it clear how to be sure that an employee won't be able to evolve.

Optimise

Your systems are the vital organs of your company, so don't just create them and forget them. Make sure every new employee has dedicated training days and a clear onboarding process where they're taught and can practise the systems. Optimising your systems is key for your company to stay ahead of the market, which moves fast. A customer's buying attitude, interest and/or behaviour is always changing.

A part of optimisation is to improve your systems as time goes by. Whenever you receive feedback that a mistake is being repeated by your teams or a process is unclear, review and correct the existing documents with the team of the relevant department(s). Add any new systems you and your team create into the right department's documentation. Act fast and get any necessary amendments to your systems sorted straight away, train the team in the new systems and always allow for improvements.

I would recommend you carry out a routine optimisation process every six months. Make sure each team and/or department revises their documents, videos and images, and updates them as needed. You could hold a team brainstorming session where employees can suggest new ways or software for doing a task, or simply what they feel is the most efficient way to do something. Look into automations, alternative software or even hiring new team members as a result of this session.

Make your expectations clear to your employees. As part of your onboarding process, emphasise how important systems are to the company. Lead by example, ensuring that you follow them as much as everyone else. You will lose employee trust and performance if you ignore the systems yourself.

You can only improve what you can measure. Your systems will give you the clarity you need to measure the performance of your company.

ACTION STEPS

In this chapter, we have looked in detail at the importance of creating clear systems that everyone can follow. This is so nobody – you included – is essential to the business, leaving everyone free to take time off for whatever reason and increasing the company's value to prospective buyers.

If you haven't already done so, now is the time to act. Start by downloading and filling in the worksheets from www.maakeacademy.com/designandgrow.

You will find:

- Customer journey worksheet
- WDW diagram

2
Team

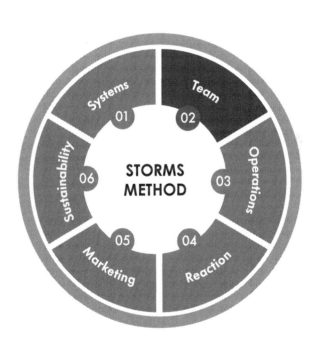

CHAPTER SUMMARY

The T in STORMS stands for team, which is the heart of your company. Choosing the right team members can have a great positive impact on your growth and revenue.

This chapter covers:

- How to build your dream team
- The importance of an organisation chart
- Employee culture and how to improve it
- Employee Strength method – PASS
- How to post a job advert to filter out unsuitable candidates

2
Team

Play nicely with others. This is what many of us were taught when we were kids. Remember those games in the school playground where the sports teacher selected two team leaders? These leaders had to choose their teams from everyone else in the class. Some leaders picked their best friend first, some picked the best player and so it went.

Now imagine you could pick from the whole school. What would your criteria for choosing be?

Have you ever heard the saying 'Business is a team sport'? The importance of team cannot be questioned for any size of business. As an entrepreneur, you are trying to create an extraordinary vision with ordinary people. The truth is that not even the top entrepreneurs of our era would have managed to achieve what they did without the support of their team.

Big corporations that have huge demands can recruit from a seemingly endless pool of talent, making candidates jump through hoops to ensure they get the top people. 'What is the secret to building a dream team?' you may ask, especially if you don't have the resources of the big players in the market. In fact, that is the most common question I get asked when talking to business owners, even those who have established a steady profitability and have systems in place.

Your dream team

One of the biggest challenges in business is building a team with one vision. A group of people with complementary skills who will work towards a common strategy and extraordinary growth that is healthy and sustainable.

You will have started your business with a vision. Putting your heart and talents into it, you'll have grown it to three, seven, maybe even fifteen people. Do you remember how hard things were when you were on your own? A founder wears many hats in the beginning and that cannot be avoided. One is the most dangerous number in business, but you escaped that trap when you started hiring your team members.

Did it all start smoothly? For many of us, building a team seems to be going well in the beginning. It's still a small team of two or three members and each person understands they will be carrying out several tasks.

As the number of team members grows, things get a little more complex. Now is when you need to get your systems in place to ensure everyone is on track. You need to be vigilant with the collection of key performance indicators (KPIs) and hold consistent meetings with your team.

There is a magic shift that happens when your company reaches a revenue of between £700k and £1.5 million. Things will likely get complicated, especially if your systems are not clear and updated. There is also a shift in the team culture. From a cosy group of friends, they become co-workers. It is an exciting if not scary time, and you need to be honest with your team and yourself about who is still a good fit for your business.

Don't think of it as judgement time where you pick out the weak links. Think of it as an opportunity for your company and your team to pursue a brighter future. The company's needs may not align with the needs of certain employees any longer. This could mean that an individual may be a better fit in a different environment where they'll face opportunities better suited to them. When you are unhappy with how an employee fits – or rather, doesn't fit – in your company, you can be sure that employee is also to some extent unhappy with their position or performance.

The transition from a small team to one of seven to fifteen employees means you need to insert the next level of leadership. Appointing new managers, coordinators and leaders becomes essential, but this can be a bit of a grey area. A lot of entrepreneurs fall into the trap of using loyalty as a reason to promote.

CASE STUDY: Dream team member to nightmare manager

This is exactly what happened to Rose (not her real name), a quiet but fierce woman who was determined to succeed, no matter what. She'd entered a competitive market in the fashion industry, but she managed to find her tribe and grow her business to employing five team members in three years. She had been sensible with her decisions and kept a close eye on the finances so far, so when she wanted to free herself from a heavy load of responsibility she could no longer carry, she decided to appoint a manager.

When we met, Rose told me how disappointed she was with her decision. She'd appointed a manager from her original team, but things weren't working out. When I asked why she had made the decision to appoint this manager in the first place, what her criteria were for making the decision, she lowered her eyes.

'She deserved it,' she said. 'She worked hard for it.'

'What do you mean?' I asked. Rose told me how her now manager had requested a meeting and made a strong case, saying how she had helped the company get to where it was and that without her, Rose wouldn't be able to fulfil the number of orders she got.

'Is any of that true?' I asked.

At this point, Rose looked me in the eyes and said, 'Some of it. She has been with me since the company was founded and is an excellent technician. She knows all the sewing machines and stitches. She is always there when I need her and I would be lost without her, but...'

Rose hesitated, then went on, 'She is a terrible communicator and not flexible at all. She wants to be left alone to make decisions and for me to be happy with all of them, and she refuses to accept any of my feedback.'

After six months in the management job, this woman wasn't getting consistency from her team. She had no data or KPIs to present to Rose, although she'd been asked to supply these, and she wouldn't collaborate on solutions. Any time she was brought in to explain why things weren't going according to plan, she would just say that she was swamped with work and had no time for these things – 'these things' being meetings, KPIs, improvements, systems, accountability, team morale, delegation and reports, all of which she had been expected to deliver. The last thing Rose wanted to do was fire her, but she knew that the woman's management style was poor, and the business was suffering because of it.

More importantly, rather than freeing up her time, Rose had to do extra work herself, including some her manager was getting paid to do. The whole situation was emotionally charged for Rose and was costing the company thousands of pounds. She had spent a lot of money training her manager and trying to shape her into the employee the company needed.

Looking from the outside, I realised it was easy for me to know what to do, but not as easy for Rose to implement it. Before getting to the point where she had to fire her manager, Rose wanted to try a few steps that we set together to prevent this outcome, even though I could see the situation was hopeless and advised against it. The last step was an employee performance review with a member of HR in attendance.

> Due to Rose's emotional guilt, she wasted a lot more money and time in training and meetings with HR, but the result was still the same. She finally fired her manager.

Why was I so sure from the beginning that Rose couldn't save the situation with her manager? Because the manager lacked certain essential qualities. She wasn't an active listener, nor was she flexible. At all. She lacked organisational skills and, more importantly, determination to respect the values of the company. With her remaining in the business, Rose would never have known what another person would have achieved with the same training *and* these qualities. Maybe she does know now.

Promoting internally due to either pressure from your employees or guilt is as costly as hiring the wrong person externally. In fact, it's even more costly, because when you promote someone into a role that's wrong for them, you lose a valued employee who was performing successfully in their previous position.

Organisation chart

This is the moment to create a hierarchy of employees and put it for all to see in a diagram known as the organisation chart. Like many (if not all) designers, I love to visualise things in my head, make connections, and then draw them out. If you do too, you're likely already picturing your existing staff shifting up and down the hierarchy in whatever form it has taken in your mind.

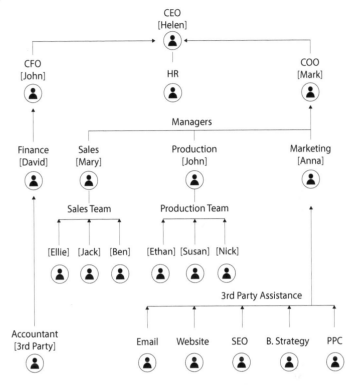

Example of an organisation chart

On the top of the chart is the CEO or founder, depending on your company structure. If there is more than one founder, decide which of you will be at the top. It is tempting to put both names up there, but this often confuses staff members. Clarity is key for your team to achieve their goals.

Ego aside, there is always one founder who is more suitable for the CEO position than the other(s). Pick the strongest visionary: the one who sees miles ahead and has a strategic mind. Continue filling up all the positions, making sure to include any external partners under whoever they report back to. You can use my model or create your own design. Designers don't waste any opportunities to create visuals, so I suspect your organisation chart will have flare. Make it happen!

Once you have your organisation chart, use it. Ensure that each team member has a clear understanding of who they are reporting to and who they can approach if they have an issue, even if that issue is with their immediate line manager or supervisor. This organisation chart should play a part in your onboarding process as well as being something your employees can refer to when they need to.

As your company grows, so should your chart. Make sure to appoint someone to make updates on this chart every three months (minimum) or more often, depending on your company growth.

In your business, you need three types of people to succeed:

1. **The entrepreneur** – the dreamer, the innovator. People like you and me who have a vision, turning the most trivial conditions into priceless opportunities. Entrepreneurial minds hardly rest; they work in complex ways and tend to process many ideas and outcomes at once. Entrepreneurs often drive others to the edge of their patience with their relentless ideas.

2. **The manager** – the organised individual who will break the entrepreneur's vision into small bite-size pieces, analyse the data and get the team to

follow through. Neat and predictable, the manager ensures everything works smoothly.

3. **The technician** – the one who will bring the vision to life. The doer; the one who knows all the technical aspects and turns the vision into reality through production. The technician knows the value of doing; that visualising and talk is great, but it won't bring results. They are simply experts in what they do.

In his book *The E-Myth*,[4] Michael Gerber explains at length the struggle the solo entrepreneur goes through on a daily basis as no one can take on three different personalities at once. For your company to run smoothly, you'll surely need to hire some technicians and managers.

The beauty of the organisation chart is you gain instant clarity on the key people you're missing and the overlap of others. It shows you an undeniable truth that you can no longer hide from. If your chart is missing a manager, that would be the first hire I would suggest you make.

Don't be their friend, be their leader

If you are anything like me, your business is like a second home. This is not because you may spend all day (and late nights) in your office (if you are doing so, we will work on that), but because you built it through your personal sacrifices. You envisioned it and you financed it; you have been through sunny days and stormy days; you love it and hate it at the same time. Your business is your baby and deserves to be loved and respected by the people who work there.

If you became an entrepreneur to make an impact in the world, you can't do this alone. You need to surround yourself with people who can lift you and your business higher. You can't be working like an octopus, dealing with several departments, answering endless questions and constantly being interrupted, or doing everything yourself because it seems the quicker and easier option than explaining a task to others. That way, you'll end up with no energy; you'll be fighting your own people to reach what should be a common goal.

Film producer Robert Evans wrote in his book *The Kid Stays in the Picture* that, 'There are three sides to every story: your side, my side, and the truth.'[5] This applies in business as it does in everyday life. You might be beside yourself with anger about a certain employee's poor performance, but once you sit down to discuss the matter, they outline their own series of complaints. Has this ever happened to you? It happens to most business owners. Every time I work with companies and conduct employee interviews to assess the strength of the existing team, I receive a high percentage of complaints from the members who the owner has marked as problematic.

When Alexander Wills and I founded maake, we set our values: honesty/integrity, teamwork, efficiency, openness to feedback and family ethos. We were proud indeed, as if by writing these values down, we would automatically transmit them into our employees' mindsets. We were a lot younger and maybe a bit naïve then.

Due to the specialised and technical nature of our business, there are a limited pool of trained employees who haven't worked for our competitors, and during interviews while we were recruiting, a lot of our candidates spoke about previous jobs. They told us how they quit because the work was too demanding; the owners were insensitive about working hours and cared little about their employees' personal lives. This couldn't be our company, we decided. We had family values, after all.

For the first couple of years, we wanted to treat the staff in a friendly, approachable manner. Alexander in particular is fairly easy-going by nature and struggles to express disappointment or frustration. Unfortunately, we tipped the scales towards being too easy-going and flexible on working hours and absences. We weren't strict and when our people made mistakes, we kept quiet about it and didn't hold them accountable. Instead, we ended up micromanaging.

You would have thought that our employees would be thrilled we were such pleasant bosses (or so we thought), but nothing could be further from the truth. We ended up creating rather than preventing tension within the workplace.

Any of that sound familiar? It is more common than you may think.

If you have children, you will know that they thrive under a schedule. Children need rules and are happy and strong when they have clear guidance; when they understand the expectations people have of them and the consequences of not living up to those. If you must change your plans with your kids, treat it as rescheduling a professional appointment. Explain why you need to postpone. You can't just assume that because you are the parent, they will have to accept whatever happens.

The same applies for all humans. We all need clarity on the expectations others have of us so we can live up to those expectations. When Alexander and I noticed that things weren't quite as we had planned them in our business, we decided to make some changes. We communicated our expectations, made people accountable and used consistency in our approach, and the results were exceptional. That's when we started to build a strong employee culture.

Employee culture

This is something that can be hard to maintain, even in the best-case scenarios. Most, if not all, employees have been in work situations where the culture was weak or even non-existent, often with pretty disastrous results for the company and its people.

What is employee culture? When founder of Apple, the late Steve Jobs, who was a visionary and an extraordinary individual, was interviewed by authors Rama Dev Jager and Rafael Ortiz for their book *In The Company of Giants*,[6] he said, '...it's building an environment that makes people feel they are surrounded by equally talented people and their work is bigger than they are... and having a culture that recruits the A players is the best way.'

For this reason, I work on my company's employee culture constantly, especially now that a lot of people have chosen to work remotely. It is more important than ever to focus some of your energy on it. There are three main points I cover.

Value your workers

There is no question that an individual who doesn't feel valued will underperform. This is as true in your personal life as it is in business. When you undervalue or ignore your partner's romantic efforts, you demoralise them. No matter how much they love you, they will be reluctant to try again and again as you seem to respond to nothing, so as far as they're concerned, you have no expectations.

The same goes for employees. When they feel that their work or effort isn't appreciated or valued, they underperform and lose interest.

Lead, don't manage. More specifically, do not micromanage. Micromanaging is the killer of employee culture.

Give them a common vision

Former CEO of Ford Alan Mulally said, 'Leadership is having a compelling vision, a comprehensive plan, relentless implementation, and talented people working together.'[7]

Without a common vision, your team members will clock in the hours, aimlessly waiting for the next pay cheque. Throughout history, leaders have led people though wars, peace, innovation and community with a simple approach: they shared their vision. It is human nature to want to be part of something bigger, something greater than oneself, and team members working in a company are no different.

Give them plenty of feedback

When something goes wrong, another thing that is human nature is to rush to point it out. No one is more guilty of that than me. I am harsh on myself and I tend to be harsh on those around me. When I taught at universities in my early years, no matter how hard I tried to sugar-coat my feedback, I had at least one student in tears – students who were only a few years younger than me. Although it was always constructive criticism, they still perceived it as harsh.

Why am I telling you this? Because I want to ensure that when you give feedback, it is welcomed by the recipient. I would aim for 80% positive, 20% negative feedback at all times. If you share a lot of positive feedback daily, when you must give negative feedback, it is likely your employees will receive it well.

You need to make it clear what your system of feedback is. Your employees should receive your feedback, take it away and digest it as they see fit; it is not an opening to further discussion, unless that is your intention.

CASE STUDY: Value your employees

When he called me, John (not his real name) had a stable business in some respects. He had won awards early in his career and landed interior-design contracts with huge names that truly put him on the map. His revenue was good and he seemed to have things in order.

When we started working together to speed up his growth, he confessed that his employees would quit after a couple of years, or they would stay, but only 'do half a job', as he put it. He had too many employees for his revenue (which meant he was cutting his profit), but still he was unhappy with the performance of some of them.

'Do you like your employees?' I asked. 'Would you go to lunch with any one of them?'

There was a silence before he replied. 'Not unless I had to,' he said.

That's where the problem begins, I thought. John had worked with these people for years and he barely knew anything about them. He didn't know about their personal lives, their interests or their ambitions. His customer relation management (CRM) software was out of date, but surprisingly, he had a deep personal knowledge of his top clients and even some of the not-so-regular ones. He needed to extend that respect to his employees.

As we moved further into the process, we discovered that not only did some of the employees not align with the company's values, but several were such different personalities that an employee culture couldn't be cultivated. After reviewing all John's systems, we started working on his onboarding so he could build a team that was totally aligned with his company values. Once these people were in place, employee culture followed naturally because John valued his people and gave them plenty of constructive feedback, they were all working towards a common vision, and everyone was supportive of the company.

Employ people you enjoy being around. Have an employee lunch once or twice every week and listen to their stories. When you know your people, you can explain your vision in a way that will vibrate with their own life goals.

The Employee Strength method

Look around you. Is your company running like a well-oiled machine with every part performing at maximum capacity? It's likely there are some areas that are problematic. There comes a point when most entrepreneurs realise that a part of their business is not making sense as it is anymore. Maybe it needs replacing, maybe it needs optimising.

When one department is not performing, the others get dragged down with it. At that point, you need to take action and consider your options.

CASE STUDY: A tough decision that gave birth to the employee strength method

During a staff meeting a while ago, I was verbally attacked by one of my employees. She had been with the company for a while, but at that point, she was furious about some of the daily inconsistencies and feeling pressured and lost.

'How hard can it be?' she yelled. 'It's just about picking up the fabric, sewing it and sending it.'

I looked at her for a while. Did she really believe that was all the knowledge entailed to complete an order? She was one of the few sewing employees and had been with the company for a long time. I knew that she felt entitled as every time a new system was presented and training days allocated, she would find some excuse to be absent or completely space out.

To get every order produced to the highest standard while the customer receives a world-class experience is extremely hard, especially with employees who believe that nothing and no one knows better than they do. Needless to say, her contract was terminated due to a number of issues, but if you want my honest opinion, it was her attitude I couldn't stand.

When I showed her the data evidencing the mistakes, complaints and refunds the company had endured because of her sense of entitlement, she was genuinely surprised. She finally understood the importance of systems and why I had been trying so hard to implement them, but it was too late.

I stayed up all night after that meeting and built my methodology for hiring team members because I never wanted to employ another person who didn't believe, appreciate and understand that what my company is doing every day is extraordinary. The Employee Strength method measures, visually and accurately, which candidates should be given a chance and who should be dismissed. It is also useful for evaluating existing employees and deciding on team fit. You can download the Employee Strength workbook here: www.maakeacademy.com/designandgrow.

There are four main stages to the Employee Strength method that form an easy-to-remember acronym. If the candidate doesn't succeed on each stage, you **PASS**:

- **P**rinciples. Hiring on values is key to maintaining your vision and employee culture.

- **A**ttitudes. Ensuring your employees have the right attitudes/qualities for the job will lead to high performance. It will also cut the cost of having several people doing a job that could be performed by one.

- **S**kills/aptitudes. Targeted skillsets and aptitudes can help your product stand out in a crowd and create high efficiency within your operation.

- **S**urplus. By calculating the return on payroll (ROP), you can determine the success of your hires. You calculate the surplus based on all employees rather than individually. You are investing in your employees, so without a high return on investment (ROI), your business cannot be profitable.

You can use this method as a base line during your interview process. Print out as many copies of the PASS worksheet from www.maakeacademy.com/designandgrow as you have candidates and use it as a consistent guide. Instead of floating notes that are time consuming and difficult to compare, this will help you make quick decisions and save time.

The number-one criterion for deciding on any hire is attitude. I am a firm believer in hiring on attitude. You can teach many things and overlook some weaknesses, but attitude is fundamental in any good hire. Unfortunately, during interviews, people have been trained to lie and show their best selves. They often know exactly what to say and how to say it to increase their chances. You will have to develop a consistently strong interview process to filter those candidates out.

Be aware that the more experienced people are, the stronger the foundations of the beliefs they are likely to have about how things are meant to be done, which allows little to no space for change. There are positions like accounting that demand an experienced figure, and others that can be taught, like machine operation, so for these roles, it is better to pick a young, enthusiastic person with little experience who truly believes in the brand. Someone who would like a career in the field is better than someone with experience with an inflexible attitude. As your revenue increases, you will need experts in most areas of your business, but until then, focus on emerging talent.

Experience and attitude are not the only things to consider. Each candidate's personality plays a significant role in their position in your company and in your life. In the book *Surrounded by Idiots*,[8] Thomas Erikson explains in detail the different types of personality and what positions they thrive in. He uses the dominance, influence, steadiness, and conscientiousness method (you can find it freely available on the web), which is a useful tool to understand people and predict their reactions in certain situations. It is also a great tool for building teams and ensuring that there is harmony in the workplace.

Principles

Hiring the right employees is an art. Your business is not Apple or Google with thousands of people knocking down your door to come and work for you, and that's OK. The first step is to know what you expect from an employee, more specifically what values you expect to share.

Think back to your dating days. You might have started dating someone, but a few months down the road, you realised that you had nothing in common. The truth is that it's your core values – those undeniable values that you were raised with or have developed over time; the values that shape who you are; the ones you would want to pass on to your children – you didn't have in common.

If you are married or have a long-term partner, think of their values. I'm sure you'll find they share the same fundamental values as you and you are both working towards a common goal (or I hope you are). If you have kids, you choose your children's schools based on values as you want them to be in a community that shares the values you hold as a family.

It's the same in business. A company should have clear, non-negotiable values that are true to the owners. They are not a collection of ideas from employees or friends; they are an extension of who you are in your professional and personal life.

Three to five values is ideal for any company. Fewer than three and the message gets lost. More than five and the values become overwhelming and confusing.

Values can mean different things to different people. When I started working with entrepreneurs, I soon realised that just stating a word or phrase, for example 'family oriented' or 'integrity', didn't have much meaning. We live in a multi-cultural environment where people have different beliefs, so we cannot expect everyone to understand our values through a single word. We need to elaborate.

If you ever visit the maake website or factory, you'll find the values explained in the web pages and framed on the walls. My favourite is the one in the toilet, because who doesn't like a bit of reading in a quiet space? This is what the explanations include:

- **Honesty/integrity:** we demonstrate honesty, openness and sound ethical behaviour in all aspects of our work, doing the right thing even when no one is watching. This is what honesty / integrity means to the owners and that's what the expectation is set as.

- **Teamwork:** being able to work in a team and collaborate efficiently with team members. Everyone must be respectful and value others' opinions and **rise together for the benefit of the business**.

- **Efficiency:** great time management. We strive to improve efficiency, effectiveness and productivity. At all times, we are respectful of our colleagues' workload and time.

- **Family ethos:** we must treat our fellow employees as family and respect each others' cultures and backgrounds.

- **Openness to feedback:** we are always open to and encourage constructive feedback and welcome the personal growth this brings.

For a happy, harmonious workplace, your team needs to be united and believe in your values. It soon becomes clear who doesn't share your core values. They are the people who frustrate you; the employees you spend the whole of dinnertime complaining about to your partner. They suck the joy out of going into work and you dread having to discuss another matter with them.

Your turn. Write down ten values you believe are unshakeable for you and your business. Here are a few to get you thinking: boldness, accountability, passion, CS, diversity, simplicity, joy/fun, quality, teamwork, trust, ownership, innovation, leadership, learning, humility. I have not given you this list for you to 'go shopping' and pick the ones that sound the best. This is not about what you hope your business to be. It is about who you are and what you can consistently deliver without fail.

Now pick your three to five core values from the ten you have written down and write a short description of what each means to you. Perfect it by using your branding to create an official document and print it out. Stick it all over the office and be sure to talk at length with your employees about what these values mean to you and the company.

Excluding certain values doesn't mean that they are not important. Picking the three to five most important ones means you and your employees can focus on those, but you will almost certainly need to use more as you move into the process of choosing your 'employees for good'. If a candidate doesn't share your values, there is no need to move any further with them. It will only end in disappointment from both ends, so it's important to include them in job advertising. That will filter out unsuitable candidates before they even apply.

Attitudes

Each one of us has our own qualities. They may be ones we've developed over the years, we've been raised with or that are simply expressions of who we are.

During different stages of life, you may want to improve on some of your qualities. It may be because you are eager to please a loved one or simply want to be a better person. If you have ever tried to change a fundamental attribute of yourself, you probably found that some are easier to change than others. Becoming an active listener, for example, is one of the hardest qualities to take on board and it needs incredible dedication and self-awareness to succeed. On the other hand, independence is something you can be taught to improve significantly.

Here, I have selected twelve attitudes/qualities which I find to be game changers in business. These will help you filter in the candidates that suit your organisation: the ones who have the core qualities to be loyal and valuable members of your team.

The qualities in bold type – seven to ten inclusive – are those that cannot be changed – not easily, anyway. You could waste time and money trying to change a candidate who doesn't have these qualities, but ultimately, you would be naïve to believe you can nurture them to become a top-performing employee.

The underlined qualities – numbers eleven and twelve – are those that can easily be worked on and nurtured in the right environment. The first six can also be learned, but only with time, constant coaching and specific guidance.

1. Reliability

2. Independence

3. Collaboration

4. Eagerness to learn

5. Self-starter

6. Self-awareness

7. **Active listener**

8. **Flexibility**

9. **Organisation**

10. **Honesty – with integrity**

11. <u>Strong communication skills</u>

12. <u>Openness to feedback</u>

The most efficient way to understand if a candidate is to be rated highly on a certain quality is to ask pertinent questions during their interview. Have a set of questions prepared and use the same template in each interview to understand how each candidate would react in certain situations. You can present a hypothetical situation or issue and ask how the candidate would deal with it.

It is essential that you have your selection criteria and questions prepared before each interview to rate the candidates fairly. On the 'Attitudes – qualities that can't be ignored' template, downloadable from www. maakeacademy.com/designandgrow, list all the game-changer qualities and use these as your selection criteria. Score the candidates from 0 to 4: 0 = poor, 1 = below average, 2 = average, 3 = above average, 4 = ideal.

Tick the quality only if the employee scores 3: above average or 4: ideal. The aim is to tick at least eight of the twelve attributes, including all the bold qualities. You can now filter down to the top-strength candidates and move to the next phase.

You can also do the same exercise with your existing team members, either in person or by delegating to your manager(s) to rate their own teams. Large corporations get team members to use rating systems to review each other to make decisions on hiring and bonus giving. Anyone consistently falling below average gets fired. This improves employee culture as well as performance. By allowing team members to rate each other, the company incentivises them to be good, thoughtful co-workers. The line manager has the final say to approve or reject the ratings (in case someone is being purposely spiteful), but this rarely happens. In fact, this works well in general.

Skills

While sitting in a café waiting for a cup of tea, you decide to order a hand-baked cake to go with it. The server is warm and polite and the cake delicious.

Your experience in this case depends on the quality of the service and the food. Would it matter if the server has a PhD or is a maths genius? Not to you. Would it matter if the cook lacks social skills and barely speaks English? Not to you.

So it is also in your business. The skillset of each role is decided by what you need from your team members in that specific role. Skills that are crucial for an accountant are not the same as those for someone working on your social media. Each time you require a new member of staff, decide what aptitudes and skills you expect them to have for the particular role.

On the Employee Strength worksheet, you will find forty-six aptitudes and skills which you can use to score your candidates against. I have included a few of these skills here just for reference.

1. Approach to risk taking

2. Experience

3. Working with numbers, words, shapes, people, data

4. Outgoing

5. **Time management**

6. **Intelligence**

7. **Analytical skills**

8. **Creativity**

9. Customer focus

10. Situational judgement

11. Empowerment

12. Self-awareness

It's the same idea as with the attitudes – numbers five to eight, the ones in bold type, are skills people either have or don't have, and numbers nine to twelve, underlined, can easily be gained with nurturing and guidance. One to four can also be developed with constant coaching and specific guidance, but it will take time.

When you set up a job description, include a set of skills that you find non-negotiable for that specific role. Focus on the skills you are not willing to train on. Your candidate must be above average on the non-negotiable skills for you to tick it off.

You can add or remove skills as you see fit for each position. Trust your original judgement and don't overlook weaknesses just because the candidate presents themselves well. If you know that a skill is essential to the role they're applying for, overlooking a weakness in it will frustrate you down the road.

You can add some secondary skills you are hoping to see that would be a bonus in the recruit. These can be skills you discuss with the candidate during the interview, explaining that training will be needed.

As with qualities, you can decide if a skill should be ticked during the interview by asking at least three questions related to the skill and observing the response. Ask for an example of how the candidate dealt with a particular situation that requires the skill in their previous job or create a hypothetical situation and ask questions about what they would do.

Surplus

It is no secret that there are two ways to increase profit. One is to increase sales and the other is to lower expenses. That's the non-sophisticated explanation you will get while chatting in any coffee shop or pub.

As oversimplified as this explanation is, there is truth in it. When you reach £1 million in revenue, payroll likely becomes one of your biggest expenses. This is often a reflection of your business being overstaffed due to employees who do a poor job. You might have hired an extra person to do the same job as someone who is not pulling their weight or be overpaying someone who isn't performing. A high-strength employee could easily replace two average ones and sometimes three poorly performing ones.

How do you know if you have too many employees? Do all your people seem essential? This is where the ROP becomes useful, because it is a number that will determine if you are overspending on salaries or have room for extra hires. It is not focused on individuals; it is based on the whole amount of the payroll of the company.

The quickest way to calculate your ROP would be to take the annual revenue – £1 million in this case – and divide it by the total amount of the salaries that you pay out multiplied by 3. Let's say that's £1,000,000 / (£303,855 x 3) = 1.10 ROP. You are aiming for 1 and above. In this case, you got 1.10, which gives a little breathing room in case you want to make another hire. An extra employee with a 30K a year salary will drop your ROP to 1. Anything more than that will drop it under 1, and that is a dangerous zone you don't want to be in.

Some entrepreneurs or big corporations like to boast about the number of employees they have, thinking it makes them look more powerful, but it is not the employee number that matters; it is the ROP. If your business has a ROP lower than 1, it's fighting for survival and you're trying to find money any way you can. You scale back, look for loans and put out fires daily. When you have a high ROP, you can scale your business, make profit, plan and focus on how to improve your operations and expand your market.

The reason you multiply your total spend on salaries by three is to get the number you would expect the employee to be bringing back into the business on an individual basis. This is not necessarily in sales as not all employees are directly linked to sales; what you want to ensure is what that position is worth to the business. This will also give you some idea what to alter in each position to make your team perform better or more efficiently.

Be mindful that your operations will also play a big role in ROP results. You can only expect the level of performance that your employees can manage with the tools they've been given. Download and fill in your ROP worksheet here: www.maakeacademy. com/designandgrow.

Once you have filled in all your Employee Strength worksheets for existing employees and calculated your ROP, you will have a better understanding if your weakness is solely in the hiring process or whether an element of operations is holding your team back. This could be anything from software to processes, morale and more.

Job posting

There are a few things to remember when you are posting an advert for a job and the top of that list is to cast a wide net. Increase your options to have the best choice of candidates possible. You can post on several platforms and contact your network to get the word out that you are hiring. Also add your job post on your website and social media.

Let's use dating as an example of the need to cast your net wide. In life, you meet hundreds of people, and yet you only date a few and even fewer become long-term partners. If you only ever met ten people, it would make your dating life frustrating as you would have to choose one of them or no one at all.

It's the same in business. When you get only a few candidates for a job, you end up picking the best of the worst, when what you want to be aiming for is the best of a high-standard selection.

The average ratio of high-performing employees to others is one to four, which means out of every four candidates that are interested in the job you post, only one will be worth talking to. Your goal is to filter out the non-suitable candidates before they waste your time in interviews. This will allow you to focus on a worthy selection.

Filtering can start as early as your job posting. Create an advert that attracts the kind of candidates you want. Think of it as a marketing campaign. You need the top talent, so you need to make the role sound attractive. Add your company's awards in the text, a description of who you are and what you are trying to achieve. Employees need to align with your values. They should feel a spark, a desire to work with you, whether it's due to the difference you as the founder are making or the company's mission. Either way, your company and the job on offer need to be inspiring and attractive.

Start with the title of the job and a job description that clearly states your expectation. Add a salary for the position – put what you are willing to pay. Do not negotiate the amount depending on the candidate, which means that you should avoid putting a range on the salary. Be specific and make sure you've tested the amount you offer on your ROP worksheet before posting the job. If a candidate feels they are worth more, wish them well and explain that they are not a good fit for your company. Getting them to accept a lower salary than they're asking for will end in resentment, which will adversely affect your employee culture. Offering them what they want will take you out of budget. Neither can have a positive outcome.

Make sure to add your core values to your job post. You only want candidates who share those values. Also add the hours or days per week the candidate will be expected to work. Explain the responsibilities of the job and the perks, if any.

When the applications come in, be sure to filter out unwelcome candidates. Those are the average or below average ones who you don't want to be dealing with at all. Get a set of metaphorical hoops for your candidates to jump through; if they are serious about the job, they will take the time to deliver.

For example, ask them to create a five-minute video on why they think they are the best fit for this position. Get them to take an online skills test so you can filter out the non-suitable candidates, which is a great way to cut down on unnecessary interviews. As your company grows, HR software becomes more and more useful. There are plenty of software options that offer online candidate assessments, but I would only recommend these for companies that have a high employee turnover or need to make a large number of important hires due to rapid growth.

Is outsourcing a good idea?

You have two options with your departments – finance, accounting, HR, IT and more. You can choose to have them in-house or outsource them. There are advantages and disadvantages to both options.

The beauty of today's market is that we live in a connected world. Technology has allowed us to spread beyond our geographical area and connect with people in different cities and time zones, removing limitations on the range of professionals we can work with. We can outsource certain jobs, meet people online and hold virtual meetings conveniently and easily. This makes it simple to use external expertise services rather than having to go through the difficulty of hiring an exceptional in-house team in a field we might not be familiar with.

There are a lot of benefits to outsourcing certain aspects of your operation, particularly parts of your accounting, IT and customer services. Customers often enjoy high levels of satisfaction when these areas are outsourced. The trouble appears when you outsource marketing. Your marketing, especially your marketing strategy, should remain within the business and be closely monitored and reviewed. Your market, your message and your product need to be breathing the same air. The way your team is built and trained and the way they pitch your product are part of how you market.

Now you've created or revised all your systems and looked closely at your team, you'll have a clear picture of where your operations are lacking and what can be improved in each department, or possibly which expertise is currently missing from your team and whether you need to hire. Whether you do it in-house or outsource it, the process of hiring should follow the principles we've looked at in this chapter.

ACTION STEPS

We have looked at building the right team or replacing existing team members if they're not aligned to the company values. We have covered the importance of your employee culture, learning how to advertise a post well to filter out the candidates who are the wrong fit with your values and recruit wisely to make sure everyone is aligned.

Now it's time to put what you have learned into action. Download and fill in the worksheets from www.maakeacademy.com/designandgrow. For the T of STORMS, you will need:

- Employee Strength workbook
- ROP worksheet

3
Operations

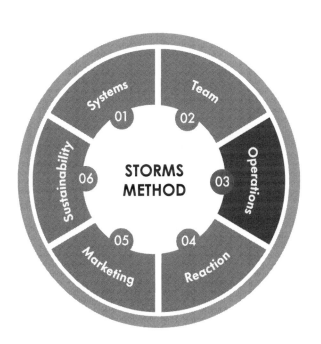

CHAPTER SUMMARY

The O in STORMS stands for operations. Increasing sales is futile if your operations are lacking, even more so if you are using materials and suppliers you are not confident with. Understanding the rhythm of your operations and fine tuning them where necessary is essential at all times, especially before rapid growth.

This chapter covers two main themes:

Daily operations, including:

- How to run team and one-to-one meetings efficiently
- CS and optimising it
- Automations and their importance
- Reducing complexity
- Shipping and delivery

The world of digital printing, including:

- Understanding inks and fabrics
- The pros and cons of digital printing
- How to pick a supplier

3

Operations

The heart of your business is your operations. That's where the magic happens.

A lot of my discovery calls start with questions about the marketing funnel. Although you might feel that marketing is the least fun and most challenging part of a business (at least for most entrepreneurs), clients usually want to jump right to it and get help to improve it. What they often don't realise is that the product's journey is just as important.

A common issue in an expanding business is a sudden growth spike or successful marketing campaign while operations are not ready to deal with it. It seems dreamy at first: orders landing in your email inbox and the numbers keep going up. That's what you want, right?

Your wish is granted; the challenge now is to deliver. Not just deliver but create a world-class experience. There is no benefit in having lots of orders if you are struggling to deliver them on time.

What if your machine has an issue, your sewing employees are sick, your packing material isn't delivered on time, the new employee still doesn't know what they are doing? Then suddenly, it seems like there are too many orders and not enough hours in the day to fulfil them. From the dreamy, you are now living a nightmare where you run around putting out (hypothetical) fires. The disappointed customers are calling day and night and an even bigger challenge lies ahead: you are put in a position where you need to deal with operational issues as well as damage control.

Delivering a world-class experience to your customer is how your business will maintain and increase their lifetime value (LTV), which is the total amount they buy from you for as long as they remain your client. The more customers return and buy again the more revenue you will produce. For this to happen, every step of your operations needs to be on track.

When you get an order, you will either receive it in your e-commerce shop or invoice it manually, depending on your sales approach and services. Once the order is placed and the invoice paid, your production team will be activated. You might have printing, cutting, sewing, upholstering or any other kind of production. Once it's ready, your dispatch team will pack the order and send it out.

To deliver a world-class experience, your team needs to ensure that each product has been through quality control and is prepared with a consistent and mainstreamed technique that is representative of your brand. Nothing kills sales faster than inconsistency: the odd mistake here and there; the messy packaging; the wrong item; and worst of all, the faulty product. Customers lose faith far too quickly and the hassle of having to make contact with your company, no matter how good your CS is, will be frustrating for them.

Your goals are to reduce complexity, mainstream processes, create an employee hierarchy and organise your space to facilitate the most efficient layout for your employees to work and circulate. I mentioned the importance of differentiating between managers and leaders in the 'Teams' chapter and I would like to reiterate that here: as your business grows, you constantly need to identify leaders and promote them to supervisory positions when necessary. By building a hierarchy of supervisors and managers, you ensure that the business results remain at a consistently high standard.

In a micro business, employees tend to wear many hats. The sewing employee fetches the fabric, cuts it, sews it, and then packs it. It makes sense then, but when your company grows, that model is no longer efficient. If your sewing team increases from two to four people, it is time to name a leader to ensure the technique and quality of the sewing is consistent. As your team grows you can appoint supervisors and so on.

Having each team member concentrating on one task tends to deliver a much better result than multi-tasking. Yes, you read that right. It's true – even if your original team members used to do more than one task and it worked for a while, it is not efficient when your business grows. From Plato in ancient Greece and eighteenth-century economist Adam Smith to industrialist Henry Ford in the early 1900s, the theories of division of labour and labour hierarchy have played key roles in the advancement of society, industry and globalisation.

Even though it may seem easier and cheaper to have one employee doing several tasks in several posts than a number of employees covering one task each and only that task, when it comes to deliverability set against salary, it actually works out more expensive due to setup and set-down costs. When many orders arrive and the demand for your product increases, the time employees waste changing tasks or posts will be noticeable as the production capacity will not be at its maximum. I am not suggesting you do time-in-motion studies on your staff (although it is a worthwhile exercise to do on your processes for positioning of tools, etc), but it is important to bear in mind the time your employees spend outside of their core role's responsibility.

Keeping your employees doing what they do best, which also decreases mistakes, avoids adding tasks to their workload that would be better done by someone with different training. Additionally, there are often many tasks that don't need a great deal of training and can be done by someone who isn't costing the business as much in terms of salary.

Imagine a heart surgeon, highly specialised and efficient in what they do, not to mention very highly paid. In the operating theatre, they focus on completing the surgery to the best of their ability. It is the hospital manager's job to give the surgeon the resources (staff and tools) that will remove any distractions from completing their goal and, of course, secure a positive outcome for the patient. The team around the surgeon may be doing something as simple as passing a scalpel, having supplies ready or wiping the surgeon's brow. Can you imagine if the surgeon had to pause his progress to rummage in a drawer for a small scalpel blade or a clamp?

You might not put someone's life at risk if your product is delivered late or faulty (depending on what it is), but repeated mistakes will suck the life out of your company and create issues that can be very costly. It is your job to maximise efficiency and reduce wastage of time, resources, money, etc by letting your team do their work. It might surprise you, but most successful business owners do not manage their processes (which you will already have laid out and approved in your systems); they lead their people and consistently optimise the employees' environment, which also optimises their performance.

Daily operations

The big picture – your vision – is the ultimate goal and to arrive there, you go through your daily operations. These common tasks are essential to the smooth running of your business, but can easily be over-looked or taken for granted. Without these tasks, you will soon find your daily operations are failing to run as well as you'd like – if they run at all.

Does that mean you need to allocate all your pre-cious time to them? It is too easy to be sucked into the daily running of the business, but remember your job is to grow the business and find time to design. Know-ing when your presence is essential, having strong systems, creating automation and reducing complex-ity will be the beginning of freeing your time.

Let's start with a task that many entrepreneurs and their teams love to hate: meetings.

Meetings

This is a word that tends to be most unwelcome in business. Do you ever feel that all you do all day is attend meetings? Meetings about sales, finances, what type of fridge would suit the team, and my personal favourite – a meeting to discuss why you are having so many meetings.

Running a business without meetings is impossi-ble. They are how you communicate with your teams and resolve issues, but they need to be controlled. As an entrepreneur, you only need to be present in a few key meetings, so train your team and allocate others to lead them. Remember what I said earlier about avoiding the temptation to micromanage your team? This is where you let them do the heavy lifting and you simply steer the ship.

All types of meetings need to be prescheduled and all attendees punctual. You and your managers need to lead by example, always being respectful of your team members' time. If the meeting is scheduled for thirty minutes, make sure it does not run over that time; use a timer if need be.

There are generally two types of meetings in business.

One-to-one meetings

These are meetings where a manager speaks in private with an employee who reports directly to them. This helps to build a strong relationship between the employee and manager and shows employees that the company leaders care about their opinion and their work. It is in this meeting that the employee reports directly to their manager and together they review the progress, successes and failing of their work in a given time, as well as allow the employee to express any concerns or struggles within the company.

The company's CEO usually holds one-to-ones with four to six employees maximum, while a manager under the CEO can handle around ten to twelve employees effectively.

There are conflicting opinions about who should take the minutes in a one-to-one meeting. Some believe that the employee should keep minutes and write them up after the meeting. This is based on the premise that it will make the employee feel more responsible and pay attention to the tasks discussed in the meeting. Some believe that the person in the higher position should write the minutes and share them at the end of the meeting, clearly stating tasks and goals.

There is a third option that works for CEOs or general managers: a secretary or designated scribe comes into the meeting to ensure all notes are documented, the scheduled time is respected and the agenda for the next meeting is completed and distributed. The scribe can also be in charge of ensuring that all tasks are completed before the next one-to-one meeting.

You and the other meeting hosts should decide what works for you all. What matters is that your team of hosts is consistent and all relevant people have access to the minutes of the meeting. A maximum of thirty minutes per employee is enough to cover all that is needed.

The thirty minutes of the one-to-one meeting should follow the 10/10/10 rule:

- Ten minutes to get to know the employee better with a few personal questions and some small talk. The goal is to create a comfortable space and eliminate any awkwardness. Your management team want your employees to want to participate and speak up about their opinions, and this is the first step to creating a safe environment for them to do just that.

- The next ten minutes is the serious bit where KPIs, goals and tasks are reviewed that the team member agreed at the previous meeting.

Recognition and comments should be made upon the team member's progress, both the employee and the meeting host giving feedback and setting new goals and tasks. If necessary, current projects and the direction of the company can be discussed.

- The last ten minutes is dedicated to the team member's performance in general. Discuss positives and negatives. If their performance is poor, it can be suggested that the remaining time is used to brainstorm solutions and their preferred ways of learning. Finally, a method should be agreed for improvement and a topic for them to focus on until the next meeting.

Team meetings

As well as individual communication, team communication about performance is vitally important. A **team meeting** can enable that by creating shared ownership of successes and failures. It is used for making decisions and announcements and giving necessary information to team members, allowing all departments a chance to express their progress and share their small wins.

Depending on your team size and the agenda, the time you'll need to schedule for a team meeting may vary. Give team members with the same level of responsibility the same amount of time to talk. This is when they share their wins and worries, improving communications between departments and allowing the members to get to know each other a bit better.

There is no rule about who should run the team meeting; in many cases as the company grows, the founder will not be present at all of them. Train a few employees to run a meeting, allowing you to choose whether to attend. Ensure that the manager of each department is present; if they're absent from work, designate someone else to take their place that day. All relevant staff members should attend.

Before the meeting:

- A member of staff should be assigned to run the meeting – known as the meeting lead – and another assigned to keep notes – the scribe.

- An agenda should be created, including all the topics to be discussed, which is accessible to all team members as soon as the previous meeting is completed. (The most common timeline is a week ahead.) Encourage employees to add topics they would like to discuss in that meeting.

- A time and place for the meeting should be clearly communicated to all employees. The place can be a physical location or online via Zoom, Teams, etc. It is good practice to have consistency on the location and time.

During the team meeting:

- The lead will welcome everyone, pass on apologies for absence and perhaps indicate who is taking a certain team leader's place, as well as sum up the minutes of the previous meeting. They should then allow for a few minutes of casual chat to get the team engaged. In our business, we often have a specific question to help the team members to get to know each other, such as 'What is your favourite drink?' or 'What is your favourite food?', which changes weekly. The lead often directs the question to specific people to avoid awkward silences. We have found that asking questions such as 'How was your weekend?' often leads to generic answers like 'Fine, thanks'.

- The lead will then introduce the main themes for discussion. Each department will be invited to share successes and issues, and actions and goals will be set as needed.

- After all departments have been covered, the lead will share the brand's highlights and successes for the period of time since the last team meeting. Upcoming changes or information might also be shared at that point. It is important to ensure that the lead always contributes last, allowing all attendees to express their opinions beforehand.

Customer service

The alpha and omega of your services pass through your CS department. This is where people communicate that they are interested in your product or have a question, seek information when there is a delay or fault, or suggest forming a partnership, but a lot of business leaders choose to have the vital CS operation as an additional task tagged on to an existing role of an in-house employee.

When your team is small, one employee can pick up the phones and answer emails when needed on top of their actual job, for example pattern making, but when your business grows, CS can't be juggled by one person. It is no longer a matter of answering a few emails and calls; your CS needs its own department with the correct software (CRM and customer satisfaction software) and trained, dedicated employees.

CASE STUDY: Outsourcing the CS operations

A while back, I worked with an interesting designer who has a kids' clothing brand that focuses on multigrow (clothes that are designed to fit for several months/ years as the child grows). Sofia (not her real name) designs the clothes and sewing patterns and her team prepares the patterns and colours for the collection. The fabrics she uses are all recycled or organic and she needs durable, long-lasting results.

When we started working together, she had a team of five with a couple of her staff answering calls and emails whenever they could. The trouble was that a lot of the calls were missed and the emails weren't organised or documented properly, although Sofia had introduced CS software.

After speaking to her team, I realised that the employees who dealt with CS were interested in sales calls, but felt that it was beneath them to deal with regular repeated questions. They had no interest in learning or committing to the software and they responded to invitations to CS meetings by rolling their eyes.

Sofia was frustrated; she knew that she was losing business and was getting calls and emails from annoyed clients, all of which she now had to deal with herself. She spent her time on damage control that was nothing to do with the product, but rather with the service.

We agreed that she would try another method. She interviewed a few top agents from abroad and outsourced part of the CS operation as a trial. Sofia was sceptical about the change at first, worried the CS quality would drop. I explained that the service had only been average at best in any case, so why not give it a shot?

The interesting part is that unlike Sofia's in-house team members, the agents were thrilled to have the job. They were so grateful and full of energy and willing to learn. After a period of training on software and systems, the agents were ready to take over the department.

Now all support tickets are accounted for and all calls are answered. There has been an increase in positive reviews online and on her surveys, and Sofia can finally concentrate on her work. The agents still need training on the sales part of the service, but that will happen over time. The important part is that all customers are now acknowledged and a personalised message is sent to each of them within minutes of first contact.

Training agents can be time consuming, so the one thing you want to avoid is making them dependent on the trainer. It is human nature to choose the easy way out and new employees often find comfort in asking questions. This is why I have placed emphasis on ensuring your employees are self-starters. In other words, you want them to find the answers themselves. If you train them and onboard them properly, there will be no need for them to require any more assistance after three months.

An effective training method I use for my own businesses – and I encourage my clients to use it as well – is the 45-minute rule: a simple rule I developed to reduce internal questions and rapidly train staff to become independent. All CS agents are encouraged to take up to forty-five minutes to search for an answer to a support ticket before asking for help from another team member. For this search, you supply a list of the relevant boards in your management software, videos and/or your CS SOPs. Agents need to be mindful not to wait the full forty-five minutes if they truly feel their search won't yield a solution.

Once they have found the answer or received assistance, agents need to deal with the ticket, and then fill in a document where they state the issue they faced. These details need to be added to the SOPs if they are not already there and discussed in the weekly CS team meeting. You should also update any public frequently asked questions if applicable so that customers have the opportunity to assist themselves without requiring help from your team.

By using this process, you can track the issues that the agents get stuck on and create more comprehensive SOPs so that issues won't occur again. What's more, should there be a turnover in staff, your systems will be more complete and make training the new recruit even easier than it was previously. Within two to three months, depending on the complexity of your services, all agents should be fully capable of tackling any issue with no help.

When they think of CS, people often believe that it's the resolution that matters. Of course, it does matter to a certain extent, but more important is the fact your customers want to be heard and acknowledged. It's the same in any type of relationship. When customers send emails or call on the phone and are ignored, no matter what their request, they get frustrated and often angry. That feeling will influence their decision whether to buy from you, buy again or not buy at all, and let's not forget the reviews. Few people leave a good review, but when they have something negative to say, they rush to their keyboard and vent their anger for the world to see.

On average, a good agent should be able to respond to 100–130 tickets a day and have an average first-response time of five to ten minutes. Listed here are a few important actions for a successful CS department:

- Ideally, use a customer satisfaction software that is compatible with and connects to your CRM.

- Ensure you have weekly reports on key support tickets that cover issues with product and service, happy customers and angry customers.

- Measure KPIs – tickets received, average first-response time, average customer satisfaction, calls received and percentage of calls answered.

- While training new agents, get them to use the 45-minute rule for at least two months.

- Set weekly goals.

- Hold weekly meetings.

- Train your team on how to handle abusive calls.

- Set clear rules for working from home.

- Make sure your working hours are clearly stated online and have automatic emails for after-hours, informing your customers of when to expect an answer.

Automations

When we set up maake, Alexander and I knew we had to do things differently. Our goal was to systematise and automate as much as possible to minimise human intervention. We were not just talking about communication and marketing; we were talking about our full production systems. But why, you might ask?

Automation is about using technology to remove mundane and repetitive parts of your business processes. It is not about removing human power, although some people believe this is the case; it is about delivering a more personalised and effective service. I would be surprised if you haven't come across automations in your daily life; perhaps you experience them constantly without even realising it.

It could be a reminder that your food shopping is on its way or an email saying you have left a product in your basket on Amazon. Technology allows for these texts and emails to be sent out automatically. Using the details the company has on record, algorithms and systems can cope with a vast number of customers and be efficient at a minimal cost per unit where humans might struggle.

As your company scales up, so does your number of customers. It is fine sending reminders to ten people a day but imagine your team having to send up to 50,000 reminders. The logistics of that, the human power required is not realistic financially or practically, and the results will be poor as mistakes will be made.

Perhaps coding and algorithms are not your thing. You are a designer and all this tech stuff gives you a headache. This might have been the case a while back, but today is an age of convenience. Software has been developed to become user friendly and efficient, even for individuals who have little to no tech knowledge. Best of all, this software is affordable.

A failure to take advantage of automations is a common mistake I see in business. The founder and the team are too busy trying to figure out their daily routine and before you know it, months and years have passed with no automation in place. Order confirmations, return labels, thank-you emails, and out-of-the-office phone messages are easily doable automations for any company nowadays.

How can you utilise automation in your own business effectively? The first step is to break down your entire operations process into granular actions. You might like first to split out the processes into the different types of operations, such as finance, sales, marketing, production, CS, etc and create a linear process map for each one. A simplified version looks a bit like this (get specific to get the best results):

Visitor on website → They purchase order → They get order email → Order goes on to system → System prints order → Team member goes to shelf and picks items → Puts them in a bag → Puts bag in a box → Ticks items packed on sheet → Goes to desk to book out shipment → Visits website to add shipping details and notifies customer → Prints label → Sticks label on package → Puts in parcel bag

The next step is to look at the individual actions and ask yourself if each one is something your team members really need or even want to do. Could it be automated? You might find that a really boring task or one that your team does over and over again or one that leads to many mistakes could be automated.

An example is the shipping label. Currently, a team member prints each label individually. What if the label could print itself? What if your software could book the order and notify the customer when it creates the shipping label, or vice versa?

Once you have a list of tasks that you would like to automate, find a way to make this happen. There are lots of great automation tools available online, from systems built into the software you already use – such as Gmail, Microsoft Office, etc – to website tools and no-code integrators such as Zapier.

Here are a few automations to help your operation processes.

- **Finance** – automate late payment reminders for customers on day seven of invoices being overdue.

- **Accounting** – integrate your website with your accounting software so all e-commerce sales are automatically entered into your system.

- **Marketing** – create automated flows in your email marketing software (more on this in the 'Marketing' chapter).

- **Sales** – create an automatic abandoned-cart email to be send when a customer leaves your website without ordering.

- **CRM** – use automation to send texts and emails to yourself or your team to remind you of customer meetings, sales and follow ups.

- **Artwork** – create an action in Photoshop to prepare a design file in ten automatic colour variations for sampling.

- **Shipping** – automatically generate a shipping label using a plug-in on your website so you don't have to type up each label manually.

- **Staff** – automatically send an email out at the end of each month to request staff feedback.

These are just a handful of the automations my businesses use, but each one takes on a job that would otherwise have to be done manually. I could probably provide another fifty for each operation but making automations work specifically for your business is key. Using the process map is a great starting point.

Developing specific automations for your own business will generate the most value to you, but it may take more time and investment than using those that are generalised. There are IT companies that can help you create automations to work specifically for your business. Although the investment might seem large up front, the long-term benefit will often outweigh the cost.

Reducing complexity

While automations are all about saving you resources (time, money, materials, etc) that can be allocated elsewhere in your business, they also contribute to reducing complexity. Complexity diverts attention and can confuse sellers, customers, and manufacturers alike.

Creating complexity in your business can be something as simple as offering fifteen designs in a pattern rather than five. This is not to say that complexity doesn't have its place, but it has to be well managed and presented in an uncomplicated manner.

CASE STUDY: Bespoke jeans

I came across a company that sells jeans, offering many versions of the same pair with options for waist measurement, thigh thickness, length of leg and colour. With three options for thigh thickness and eight different lengths, you get twenty-four variants of the same pair. Now adding the six waist sizes available for the jeans, that's 144 pairs of jeans that need to be in stock for a single sale of each variant.

That was just for one style and colour; the company had many more options. From a customer's point of view, it is fantastic to have the choice to buy the exact size, and once they have the right fit, they can purchase with confidence in other styles and colours. However, the company runs the risk of the sale not going through because the customer gets overwhelmed by the amount of choices they have to make and a high volume of returned items as customers order several combinations to find the perfect fit. They will have to order many pairs (if they can afford to), try them on and send back all those that are unsuitable. Yes, the company may sell one pair of jeans, but it will have to cover return costs, pay staff for quality checks and ensure the returned product is ready to be resold.

In this case, the company leaders have decided they are willing to pay these expenses. They believe that the complexity is worth it as each customer will have a high lifetime value (LTV) as they will know their exact size and preference for future purchases.

You need to think carefully about the amount of complexity you offer on your product with reference to your business model. Stock will no doubt be a key concern, but more than that, customers can get so excited by choice and even overwhelmed that they can't make up their mind and leave the decision for later. Later becomes never and sales drop.

At maake, at any given time, we hold around 150 fabric base types, and these can be printed in approximately twelve varying sizes with either a customer's own design or one of 10,000+ designs on the website. There is a fair amount of complexity in the production process, especially when we combine manufacturing on different machinery, so it wasn't easy to make it smooth, and it took money and time to build robust systems based on long-term structured planning. Automation along with deep relationships with our supply partners has helped us handle this complexity.

Even though we have a healthy working model, I still work diligently to reduce complexity, simplify the customer journey and curate the designs to help customers make decisions quickly. It is an ongoing process that needs constant attention; it cannot be done once and forgotten.

There are common issues that arise when you add complexity to your operation alongside short-term production cycles or planning for seasonal changes. Taking on new production partners or handling many of them at once can be tricky. Inconsistency in quality and complex steps for customers to take can lead to them losing confidence and trust in the business, especially if you can't deliver or there is confusion as to what you are offering.

It's important for the customer to identify your product or service as the best match to solve their problem or fill their needs. I have worked with lots of successful businesses that simplified their product range or offerings so their customers could understand what they were after. You can do this by analysing your sales and production. Identify which products barely sell and which cause the most issues in your production, then cut them off. It is better to focus on a few of your highest-quality products that sell well rather than have a range just for the sake it.

I am not saying that you shouldn't develop new products and expand your range; I am saying do it strategically and only after you have found a successful way to produce and deliver your key products. By carving complexity out of your business, you claim time, money and efficiency back.

Complexity can be due to your price range. When you sell many products at a low price, you will need to fulfil more orders. Your production team will be extremely busy, you will be paying more salaries, have more problems and need more CS. To make £1,000, you will need to sell 100 T-shirts at £10 each. What if you sold ten T-shirts at £100 each instead? You will be producing and packing either 100 T-shirts (and dealing with 100 customers) or ten T-shirts (and dealing with ten customers).

If your company doesn't have massive investments and is growing on its own merit, you need to consider the subject of pricing carefully in relation to the complexity and production of the business. Your product price plays a large role in your operations and their complexity.

Results

You and your team can walk on solid ground, knowing where you are at all times, but this can only happen with a clear view of results. Actions and results – that's what business is all about.

I am not referring to general results such as total revenue that increases or decreases. Those indicators are useful for the big picture, and the CEO and chief operating officer (COO)/chief finance officer would have to discuss the large numbers, but for them to get those numbers, everyone in the company needs to play their part.

Insist on accountability and ownership from each team member over their role. The way to true accountability is with KPIs, which are measurable numerical results that indicate the success of a task or activity. Examples of KPIs are the number of orders placed, the number of orders fulfilled, the number of customers calling and the number of complaints by phone in any given day.

When you know these numbers, you can take action. You can set goals, or ideally get your managers to do it, and review them on a weekly and monthly basis. KPIs for your strategy team need to be reviewed every three months and six months accordingly.

For example, you can determine the numerical goals you and your team want to achieve in sales numbers, revenue, decrease of faults, increase in sustainable products in your range or anything that you all consider critical to the bigger picture and the direction you expect the brand to go to.

The aim is always to have an overall view of your company. This way, you will know how well it's doing and be alerted within weeks of things not going according to plan, in which case you can take timely drastic action. Best of all, you will easily be able to identify where the issues are occurring. When you see the complaints or faulty item numbers in the KPI rising and you know who is sewing those items – because, of course, you have a system that allows you to document that – you can resolve this before your customers lose trust in your product.

As we saw earlier in the chapter, team managers and members set goals during their meetings, some of which can be based on the KPI analysis. For example, it might become apparent from the KPI reports that the number of faulty items delivered to clients during the previous week was high. During the meeting, the issue will be raised and goals will be set.

If last week customers received ten faulty items, this would involve two teams: production and quality control. The ultimate goal is to have zero faulty items delivered to the client, so each team will have its own goal. The production team will need to aim for fewer than five faulty items (a realistic starting point with regards to the complexity of production), and then quality control will have to aim to spot all faults before moving the orders to the next stage, allowing zero faulty items to get through to delivery for the coming week. The goal is now clear and the teams know what to do.

In the table below are a few examples of KPIs for different departments to get you started. Your brand needs a set of results that are important to you, but you don't want too many as you don't want to increase complexity.

Sales KPIs	Website KPIs	CS KPIs
Revenue	Unique visitors	Tickets received
Unique orders	New unique visitors	Average first-response time
Unique customers	Returning unique visitors	Average customer satisfaction
Orders per customer	Conversion rate	Calls received
Average order value	Bounce rate	Percentage of calls answered
SEO KPIs	Email KPIs	PPC KPIs
Page views	New email opt-ins	Ad spend
Organic page views	Active subscribers	Revenue
Blog traffic	Active in the last 90 days	Return on ad spend (ROAS)
Blogs published	Unsubscribes	Number of conversions
Content upgrades	Revenue from emails	Conversion rate
	Email campaigns sent	Cost per click (CPC)
		Cost per conversion

Examples of key KPIs

Shipping

Shipping is a key operation of any business that is selling a product or saleable service, as this is about delivery. It is about making sure that the customer receives the product as intended. More than anything in my experience, it is about managing expectations.

It all begins pre-shipping. The customer should be able to see clearly which day and time(s) to expect their product to arrive, so you need to trust the companies you partner with for shipping to be reliable. It is important to use a premium service provider such as UPS or DHL over a lower-level courier that simply leaves the parcel on the customer's doorstep after chucking it around the depot.

Rush shipping is a big part of our changing world. Everyone seems to be in such a hurry that customers often pay a high price for delivery to ensure they receive the product within one to three days. The price for rush shipping is determined by the courier you use as well as the extra hours or expense it might take to prioritise certain orders. You can use automations and the correct software to organise the orders and ensure your team doesn't need to figure out manually which to prioritise.

Even after years in business, I still find it exciting to receive a package containing the new labels or designs my company has developed, or even a new pair of scissors. Every customer awaits the moment they receive a parcel, and their first impression of your company depends on your packaging and your product.

The first impression is not the only one that counts. Every subsequent impression the customer gets must be of an equal or higher standard. This is not only about your product itself, but also about the services you use to deliver it – i.e., the shipping company's care and responsibility to deliver your product on time and in a beautiful condition.

Companies often overlook post-shipment communication with the customer, but emails or text messages about tracking the parcel help smooth the process. This also helps your CS team to be efficient at resolving issues and preventing complaints.

Shipping is a reliable low-cost marketing and sales opportunity, so why not send a support email on how to use the product or follow-up product suggestions or a customer survey? You could also get a team member to call to ensure the parcel has arrived and everything is according to the customer's expectations. You might even include in the package a brochure to inform the customer of other products or services you offer or a discount card to encourage another sale.

The world of digital printing

Part of your daily operations is manufacturing – something I am particularly passionate about. If you love fabric, I'm guessing you are as excited about the endless possibilities of digital printing as I am. That is the secret ingredient in your product and the better you understand it, the easier production will be.

There are several methods for reproducing designs on textiles, which include digital, lino, rotary, foil and screen printing. I will be focusing on digital printing as it's the technique I have the most experience with. It is also the most environmentally friendly of all the commercial techniques.

With digital printing, you can have more possibilities, more fun and more sales due to its versatility. Knowing your fabrics and understanding the techniques of this kind of printing can separate you from your competition, strengthening your marketing, message and the quality of your product. If you are not yet using fabric, hopefully this will open your eyes to new opportunities.

What is digital fabric printing and why has it become so popular?

Textile dyes have been around in various forms since 30,000 BCE.[9] Cloth coloured using natural dyes was historically mainly the preserve of aristocracy and royalty, who desired something colourful and different, until the mid-nineteenth century when synthetic dyes were discovered.[10]

Colours and patterns always catch the eye, so designers around the world have embarked on a journey of numerous possibilities. When you watch a fashion show, look at your cushions, your sofa, your curtains, even your kitchen apron, you see brilliant designs on flowing fabrics. Some of those fabrics have been digitally printed. You want to know how?

Digital textile printers are similar to your inkjet printer at home: they have sets of inks and are fed fabric on rolls instead of paper. Once the fabric comes out, there are different finishing techniques depending on the chosen process. Some inks are designed for baking or fixing through massive machines that are burning hot, while others get steamed to activate the dyes before the fabric is washed in various baths of water. The different processes result in different implications – to the product, to your wallet and to the environment; costs that must be considered when picking your fabrics.

For many years, manufacturing personalised or intricate products carried a heavy cost – mainly due to the large amount of time, expense and skill required to engrave the flat or cylindrical rotary screens used in industrial printing machines. To visualise how these screens work, imagine a detailed version of the potato stamps you make as kids. To screen-print on fabric, each colour requires its own screen. Therefore, when you needed multiple colours, you required multiple screens, resulting in a compromise between the number of colours/complexities of your design and cost – not to mention the huge minimum numbers needed to run the prints. As technologies have advanced, machinery and software have become more affordable and commercially acceptable, allowing factories to open their doors to smaller brands and designers, and offer affordable shorter runs with no minimum orders and far more possibilities.

Let's get a bit more technical. Digital textile printing is a versatile method best used for reproducing detailed images and patterns, photographs and complicated designs. Its strength lies in offering endless possibilities for colours and designs at no extra cost due to the fact that there is little to zero setup required. The base material for digital printing is usually white, ecru or ivory to enhance the design detail and colours. This doesn't mean that you can't experiment with coloured fabrics but be mindful that just as you would see a change in the colour of your inks while drawing on coloured paper, you will also see it on coloured fabric.

Typically, the number of inks in digital printing ranges from the four process colours of cyan, magenta, yellow and key (black) (CMYK) to between eight and twelve colours. These additional colours will add to and expand the gamut (the range of colours the machine is able to produce on that specific material), which allows complex designs to print more accurately.

Depending on the number of colours your supplier uses, your print will look different. This is one of the reasons sampling is essential before you print your collection. The wider the gamut, the greater the ability to reproduce fine tones or hit specific spot colours or outlying bright colours.

Some printers may use orange, blue, green, red, etc to improve the strength of certain shades, and light colours such as light magenta or light cyan to improve skin tone gradients, or greys and blacks to help with black tones. Some machines even allow the addition of fluorescent colour channels, but currently with digital printing, you are unable to print metallic colours.

Designers tend to love the limitless possibilities of digital printing for designs, colour tones and scale. Once the design is submitted, it is run through a software called a raster image processor (RIP) that converts the digital images to colours for each ink channel (colour), effectively creating digital screens using very fine dots.

The two main types of digital textile printing are:

- Direct-to-textile, which is predominantly used for cotton, silk and linen-based fabrics as well as some human-made fabrics

- Sublimation (transfer paper) printing, which is used only for human-made base fabrics

Both methods use similar or even the same machinery with slight modifications to allow and optimise variance in material handling. The results are high-quality designs produced quickly with excellent results. Due to the quick turnaround, these methods are highly relied upon for fashion shows, theatre production, movies and many brands that want to reduce stock holding or experiment with bringing collections directly to the market instead of taking the risk of holding massive stocks.

How safe are digital printing inks? The answer is extremely safe. One of the biggest markets for digital printing is kids' wear and kids' safety is a number-one priority. The vast majority of digital textile inks are water-based and will meet Oeko-Tex certification and registration, evaluation, authorisation and restriction of chemicals (REACH) requirements. These are the two most important regulations for safe chemicals.

What fabrics are used for digital printing?

A world of endless possibilities. Depending on the supplier you choose, you can pick from their range or, in some cases like maake for example, you can even provide your own fabrics. You will need to check with your supplier if they provide that service. If they do, send a sample of your chosen fabric.

Be mindful that fabrics with loose threads or long hairy fibres don't react well to direct digital printing. The print heads are very close to the fabric during the print process, so if the fabric is not suitable, it can easily damage them. No experienced factory will accept an order for an unsuitable fabric. Also, loose fibres and threads on the face of the fabric give a poor result. After they fall, you can be left with hairline blanks all over your print.

Are you still with me? I hope I haven't got too technical for you. Next up, it's fabric types.

The main fabric types used in digital printing are cotton, linen, silk, nylon and polyester:

- Cotton is a natural fibre that's ideal for clothing and is used extensively in the fashion industry and home interiors. It's a popular and long-lasting choice.

- Linen and linen-blend fabrics are also plant-based and are used for various products, such as upholstery, handbags, quilts and clothing.

- Silk is another natural fibre that takes well to digital reactive or acid printing. It's popular for fashion garments or accessories.

- Polyester, which is human-made, is now used in more than 50% of the world's fabrics.[11] It is extremely versatile – polyester can be used in nearly all applications, from fashion and interiors to the motor and display industries. Polyester is now also available as a recycled option (rPET).

- Nylon fabric is predominantly used in interiors, swimwear and outerwear – uses where fibre durability is required.

Each fabric has its unique look and brightness when it prints. Cottons and linens take on a deep look in colour, which makes them perfect for classic styles in pastel shades. Polyesters have a bright, intense look, which remain bright and strong after washing and handling. When you choose your fabric, always sample the design you intend to use to test how it prints. You will find the same design file prints differently on each fabric; this is because the ink will enter the fabric blend in a unique way, depending on the weave, density and thickness.

Fabrics that are mixed (from a blend of both man-made and natural fabrics, excluding lycra) are not generally recommended for printing digitally as the inks can react with one type of fibre more than the other. This results in the inks not bonding to certain mixed fabrics, causing an inconsistent and uneven appearance, which is less than desirable.

The inks play an important role in your decision on the type of fabric you'll use. For instance, you cannot effectively print on a polyester-cotton mix under 80% polyester with sublimation inks, as the inks will only bind to the polyester fibres in the fabric. On the other hand, with reactive dyes, you cannot print on fibres that are not natural. Acid dyes will not work on cottons; they only work on silks, wools and polyamide.

In most cases, fabrics require special preparation to be printed. That's why picking a knowledgeable, reliable supplier can make a big difference to your product.

Advantages and disadvantages of digital printing

There are many advantages to digital printing, which is what makes this process so popular. Printing as much as you need when you need it is expanding the possibilities as it has reduced stock hold and waste. Other advantages include:

- Reproduction is consistent throughout the run.

- Detail is clear and precise.

- The process is relatively inexpensive compared to other printing methods.

- You can print a single design or a short run.

- The cost isn't affected by the number of colours used in the process.

- You can customise designs – including the scale, orientation and size.

- The ability to print complex, intricate designs such as ombré patterns with ease.

- Reproduction quality stays the same, even if you only print some now and others a few months later.

- You can order a sample first to see the results cost-effectively.

- Set up and production can be extremely fast with fabric printed in a matter of hours or even minutes.

Disadvantages to consider:

- Most machines cannot currently reproduce white within the print.

- You can't replicate Pantone colours that match those on your computer screen or printed paper; you need to use your supplier's method of colour mapping. At maake, for example, we use a colour atlas, which allows you to select from 2,500 colours to match your design. Each supplier will have their own way to help you match colours, which may vary in number depending on the supplier's production possibilities.

- Inks do not always pass through the fabrics well, which makes printing on the reverse look less intense. This is not much good for items like scarves. Screen printing gives a full bleed through to the other side of the fabric.

- You can't use metallic colours and fluorescent fabrics are much harder to process.

- This method is more expensive for large simple print runs than screen printing.

- It does not effectively print on dark-coloured fabrics.

How to pick a supplier

You want to find the right supplier, depending on your needs and those of the particular project. Experienced suppliers will help you make the right choice of fabric and often offer artwork help services, too. A supplier can be temporary or last a lifetime.

It used to be common sense for brands using around 800 metres a month on digital printing to source their fabric from a 'cheap' market. Product developers would visit countries such as China, Turkey and India and fight the language barrier to cut some type of deal. Initially, this all seemed to go well and, apart from a few issues, things ran smoothly. Buy stuff from China and have it delivered. Simple.

If containers shipped without delays and prices stayed low, why not keep outsourcing to these markets? Aside from the obvious language barriers, cultural issues and travel expenses, supply chains have been breaking down since 2019, and they are getting worse and worse every year. Political and social issues have affected the market greatly and we are all now faced with the dilemma of what to do next.

There are several reasons why production is reshoring to the UK. For your brand to stay relevant, you might want to ride that wave or risk being left behind. As manufacturing in the UK becomes consistently more automated and affordable, cheap labour becomes less of a factor. You no longer save anything by using lots of cheap labour versus slightly more expert labour incorporated with automation. These factors are driving the quality, price and reliability. Consider this when you are buying fabric, or any other product for that matter.

Ultimately, it used to be that the quality, price and reliability overseas were all way better than buying from a UK manufacturer, but recently, the quality has dropped, the price has gone up and the reliability has decreased, and everyone is looking to bring production back home. One of the biggest problems I hear from customers who are bringing their production home is that they are fed up with the minimums required by overseas manufacturers. Sure, the prices may be slightly cheaper in the short run, but a huge consideration to take into account that it's not what you sell, but what you are left with. In this day and age, with the speed of turnover of products, you might never be able to sell those items profitably, or by the time they arrive, they will already be outdated or someone will have released a similar product and taken the market share. Then you have your money tied up on your shelves where it can't be spent else-where. Reaction time is everything.

I have seen customers saving up for months to be able to place a big enough order for overseas produc-tion, then having to wait another four to five weeks to receive the fabric. Apart from anything else, this is not a modern way of doing business. The matter of sus-tainability cannot be ignored, and the human cost of paying people absurdly low wages abroad in order to produce goods for the UK. We'll expand on this topic at length in the last chapter, but it goes without saying that this is a big part of the decision-making process for every brand.

You have to figure out what is important for you, but this list covers the main things, in my experience, that most brands want from a supplier:

- **Supply security** – your brand (along with everyone else's) needs a secure supply chain. When you require a product, you want to know that the supplier will be able to deliver it.

- **Consistency in quality and price** – consistent quality can make a world of difference to your product. You feel comfortable that you know what you are getting, that your product has been tested and there will be no surprises. Price is also an important consideration that can be influenced by many factors. Your suppliers are affected in the same way as your brand by political and social matters, but as long as the supplier's prices are reflecting the service you get, this can be less relevant to your decision.

- **Product integrity** – you want your brand's values to align to an extent with your suppliers'. The product should be ethically sourced, the supplier needs to have all the relevant certificates and they must be able to answer your questions easily.

- **Assurance of sustainability** – none of us can exclude sustainability from our decision making any longer. Your supplier should follow measures of sustainability and show some interest in improving their services and aligning them to the changing world.

- **Reliable information and data** – communication on products and information is a priority when you commit to a supplier. You need to be able to access and understand all the data that will inform your decision without a lot of effort.

ACTION STEPS

You have a lot to think about after having read this chapter, which has covered two themes: daily operations and digital printing. Here's a recap of the action you are now ready to take:

- Assign a team member to set regular meetings for all employees and teams.

- Train your managers on how to run a meeting efficiently and create a meeting agenda.
- Implement the 45-minute rule for your new hires and existing staff.
- Identify three to five automations you would like to work on in the next four months.
- Investigate the complexity of your business model and come up with three ways to reduce it.
- Set KPIs and ensure all members fill them up weekly, monthly and quarterly.
- Pick the method of digital printing that suits your brand and ethos.
- Revisit your suppliers and ensure you are getting what your brand needs.

4
Reaction

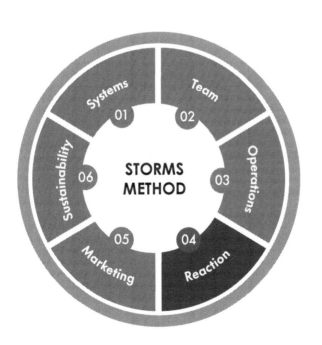

CHAPTER SUMMARY

The R in STORMS stands for reaction. Who you are and how you react in any situation often depends on years of conditioning. It is a very difficult process to change old habits, but when you succeed, you will discover your business has many rays of light shining on it. You will be able to act and react in all situations with the strength of a true leader.

This chapter covers:

- Your struggle to keep your vision in sight
- How to claim your genius zone back
- Why your brand is all about *you*
- How to stop holding yourself back – you have what it takes
- Why you get back what you invest

4
Reaction

While at a friend's party, I walked around and chatted with the guests, and I realised something. Many of them referred to themselves as entrepreneurs, but in reality, they were just business people.

How can I say that? These people are running their own businesses, so shouldn't they be free to use the title entrepreneur? The title doesn't really matter… except it does. It limits their ability to face the truth about their business.

Of all the people I have known or worked with, only a few were real entrepreneurs from the start. You and I started with a dream, a vision; the excitement of planning couldn't be contained anymore inside of either of us and a business was born.

This excitement, this desire to realise a vision hits people at different stages in life. Perhaps it's when our partner is pregnant and we suddenly need stability, or the day our boss holds one overly long, boring meeting too many. It could be for any reason or no reason at all, but the idea matures until we realise we can no longer work for someone else. After all, whatever we do for them, we are damn good at it, so why not break away and become successful?

Suddenly, any respect and admiration we had for our boss fades. Do they even appreciate us? We are better than they are, we can do better. How hard can it be, after all, to run a successful business?

If you're coming from a background of full-time employment, whatever you have been doing in your previous job, there is no doubt you are talented at it. In fact, you are excellent at it, but it is technical work. There is an element of stability in it. When you are working for someone else, you know that when your shift is over, work is done for the day.

When technicians start their own business, they tend to make one crucial mistake. They believe that because they know how to deliver excellent technical work, they will be just as good at running a business. Then the business slowly expands and before they know it, the team has grown.

When you're moving forward with your own business, this is when your *reaction* to things starts to change. You are a fashion designer, a pattern maker, an interior designer, yet you have no time to design any more. You almost certainly started this venture because you wished for freedom – freedom of expression – recognition and success, but when you look around, all you see are piles of forms to fill in, a full calendar and an empty wallet. This last issue could be because you keep reinvesting in your business or you have hired too many staff who don't deliver or simply because your cash flow is not organised the way it should be.

The freedom you once sought is a distant dream. Instead, your business is now a trap that holds you hostage. Work is no fun at all; the vision has turned into terrifying problems and lots of ifs. You have heard it all – all the terminology, the blogs on sales, the marketing strategies – and yet you care little about repeatedly going over things that frankly don't interest you.

If that's the situation you are in, it's time to seek help. I hope the first three chapters of this book have placed you in a better position to be aware of your company's weaknesses and you have already taken actions to remedy some of those issues. On the other hand, you may still feel completely overwhelmed and keep thinking that you can't handle any more work. All you want is your vision and your time to design back.

Claiming your genius zone

Even the best entrepreneurs get sucked into the trap I have just described and it's hard to get out. I should know – it happened to my business partner.

CASE STUDY: Where did my vision go?

I went into business with Alexander Wills because he is brilliant at what he does. He was raised as the third generation of his family legacy in the textile industry and has more than eighteen years' experience where he's made his own mark. No one I've met loves fabric more than he does. He has a true passion and it's really something to see when he gets in the zone.

Alexander was a well-established operations manager when we first started out in business together, but he also had the entrepreneurial bug. Shortly after the business took off, though, I noticed that he was losing his enthusiasm. He was stressed and overwhelmed. Did I mention he also has a degree in accounting and finance and an MBA? The thing is, that even with all his knowledge and abilities, he'd slowly lost his way and was spending all his time on all sorts of matters rather than on what really mattered. Our vision was fading in his mind as he went in and out of the factory, putting out daily fires.

Luckily, he wasn't alone. By working together, we found it easy to see that he was allocating his time to things that didn't concern him – matters that needed to be delegated to others and not dealt with by him.

'Do you value your time?' I asked him one day. 'Do you want to be home with your family for dinner?'

'Of course,' he said, 'but I have all these tasks to finish, and then some more.' There was no doubt he worked harder than anyone, but his endless efforts didn't mean he was creating a better business.

'We are a team, remember?' I told him. 'We will do this together. This is why we started this business as a team: to help each other when we strayed off the path.' I then presented him with a time analysis sheet (you can download one here: www.maakeacademy.com/designandgrow) and we worked on it together to get his entrepreneurial spirit back.

Each business owner must own their genius zone. Do you remember yours? It is the thing you excel at and enjoy the most. The beauty of being the owner of the business is that you can be an entrepreneur *and* a technician (to an extent), as long as you find a balance.

Think of a movie being made. You've got actors, a cameraman, screenwriters, someone handling the lights, assistants, assistants of assistants, make-up, hair, people who pick the clothes, people who dress the actors and so on. There are so many jobs on a set, it is hard to keep up with all of them, and yet the crew is so co-ordinated, they arrive and jump right in.

Who is the one they all look up to, get instructions from? The director. The director walks in, does their thing and walks out, delegating tasks and giving instructions and guidance.

Can you imagine Tim Burton going around and helping get the set built? The lighting done and the food prepared? That would be a waste of his talent and a total waste of his time, not to mention a waste of money. Your time is just as precious and you shouldn't trade it easily.

Time sheet

'Time is money,' said Benjamin Franklin.[12] Although that's true, it is a lot more than that. Your time is limited, and it should be allocated to what you love doing. Optimise your day to make the most of it in your business and personal life.

I mentioned a time sheet in the case study and here is why. The idea is to identify where you allocate your time during the day and what you allocate it to. It is a way of finding your genius zone and focusing on your strengths while delegating your weaknesses to your staff.

The time sheet has four actions:

1. **Execute** is when you do something yourself. It refers to any action that you execute, whether it's your job or not. This will include meetings.

2. **Assign** is when you pass tasks on to others during the day, briefing them on what they need to do. It's also when others come to you to get clarification on an assignment that they have been given. You are the one in control here. You are the director who will walk them through exactly what they need to do and how.

3. **Delegate** is your golden phase, so cherish it. You assign tasks and ensure your employees take ownership of those tasks. The reason I am not using the world 'accountable' in this case is because accountability is not the same as ownership. Ownership is more than just knowing

what you need to do to achieve a result; it is about feeling responsible towards something that is assigned to you. It refers to an internal responsibility. You will get credit for doing the task well and be held accountable if you don't do it, not because someone has pointed a finger at you, but because everyone knows it is your area/job.

4. **Design** is your entrepreneurial moment. You are designing the future of your company, working on your ever-evolving vision. Your team is well equipped to do their tasks and they only need to be briefed at your weekly meeting.

You will need to fill up at least five days' worth of data on your time sheet before you will be able to analyse it. After you complete the sheets, you can group the results and see where all your time goes. It will likely become apparent that you spend way too much time on **assign** and way too little on **design**. The aim is to consciously shift things and **delegate**, clear your day to make space for more design time. **Execute** should cover your genius zone, whether it be sales or designing collections. It's whatever you love doing and do best.

As your business grows, you will need to spend more time *on* your business and not *in* your business. Working on your business includes developing growth, building strategies and partnerships, strategic planning, looking for funding if necessary, financial projections, research and perfecting your pitch. Working in the business is about day-to-day activities that you can easily delegate to a team member. This includes operations, admin work, team training, marketing and sales execution, delivery of the product and CS.

When you have the data about your daily routine, it's time to remove anything that shouldn't be part of your working day. It is essential to get your team to do the time sheet exercise as well to ensure that each member is using their best skills and not wasting time on tasks that are under their pay grade or ability.

It's all about *you*

When you wake up in the morning and head to the shower, your first thoughts of the day occur. Perhaps your dreams and fears flood your mind. Then you get out of the shower and look in the mirror. Who is that looking back at you? Do you feel confident and powerful this morning or fearful and unsure of what the day will bring? What life will bring?

Being an entrepreneur is exhilarating, but it is also scary and challenging. You started with a dream, a vision, a purpose, but sometimes it feels like the walls are closing in on you. But why do you feel this way? Is it the business or is it you?

Old habits die hard

From a young age, we are usually told what to think or believe. Our view of the world is shaped by our family and those around us; by the experiences we have while growing up as well as our family's situation, religion, and ethnicity. I have seen it in loved ones and I have seen it in myself. The way others treated us in high school, university and our previous or current relationships has left a mark and often this is hard to erase.

Life is unpredictable and what we were once taught as a social norm proves to have no bearing on our lives as we grow up. Remember those top students who got all the awards and were labelled smart? Those first to be picked for the school sports teams; those who had all the friends and looked like the world was just going to unfold perfectly for them? Remember the quiet people, the weird-looking ones who everyone made fun of? Maybe even you thought they were dumb.

Life has proven how wrong we all were. There's no need for reunions anymore; we only have to check Facebook and Instagram and LinkedIn posts and TED talks by successful people from our past whose names we barely remember. Suddenly, so-called 'dropouts' and 'lazy' people seem not so dumb or lazy after all. We thought some were socialisers who would waste their life, but they didn't – they are now in respectable professions and have happy, stable families.

This is a clear message that what Dad or Grandma said wasn't quite true. Regardless of popularity and academic and sporting successes at school, a mixture of people rise and become successful in business and life. Hard work and studying are not always what takes you places in life; it's all about what you believe. It's about working smart, not working hard.

I have met many successful entrepreneurs who didn't bother with a degree. Degrees and studying don't make you successful, at least not in the way people sometimes think they do. Studying opens up your mind to experiences, people and a way of viewing the world and your work, but it doesn't guarantee success. That comes from you: from your mindset, your skills, and your reactions.

Mindset matters

You might have been top of the class and felt that you were destined to make it as you ticked all the boxes, or you might have been labelled a dropout at school, but now you truly love what you do. Either way, your mindset is what will set you apart from others and determine if you make it or not.

The human mind is designed to desire. We use images and information we have absorbed in our daily life and create our ideal scenario. Children are a perfect example – they only know what they know, and their wants and desires are derived from that. If they have never tasted chocolate, they will never desire it, so won't endeavour to get it.

It is the same with adults: our thoughts become things. Our desires and goals are created from a combination of images we have seen: a large house pictured in a magazine; the lifestyles of the rich and famous; a magical wedding and so on. The difference between kids and adults is that kids say what they want while adults often express what they *don't* want.

Let's take a hypothetical situation. You're at work, dealing with quality control, and see the same mistakes again and again from one particular employee. You call them into a meeting and tell them that you don't want to see any more damaged goods going out to delivery. It's like saying you are expecting mistakes; you just want to stop them from being delivered.

What if you approached your meeting in a more productive way? Explain that you expect to see perfect products and the faults will need to decrease by 30% by the end of the week. Now, you are giving positive feedback and setting your expectations. You are controlling the way you react to the situation.

I once watched an interesting experiment in a parenting workshop.[13] The people leading the workshop picked a group of parents and stood them in three rows. Then they simply told them what *not* to do.

For example, 'Don't sit down.' Half the parents sat, and then got up; some took a few seconds and didn't move; most made a tiny bounce, and then stayed standing. 'Don't talk.' Many blank faces. 'Don't clap.' Lots of fingers moving.

In a second round, the parents were told what to do. 'Stand up'; 'Stay quiet'; 'Keep your hands apart'. When the parents were asked afterwards to describe their experience, they all admitted that it had been way harder to follow the negative commands than the positive. They had to do double the work because even though their brain told them to not do it, the idea still lingered.

'Don't think of a pink elephant.' Ha! Bet you just did.

The idea of empowering your brain with direct instructions is a major foundation to a healthy mindset. 'I don't want my business to fail' is a classic example of anxiety and fear. If your mind is occupied with debt and failure, you see it everywhere you go. Believe that you will succeed, that you will get all your invoices paid and will double your sales in three months, and your mind will set its course for that. You will be working towards that; your energy will be focused on setting you up for success.

Mother Teresa is reputed to have said, 'If you hold an anti-war rally, I shall not attend. But if you hold a pro-peace rally, invite me.' She knew that we should be focusing on what we want – peace – and not just standing against war. You need to truly understand the distinction between the two, as it makes a major difference to the outcome. This is not about wishful thinking or magical change; it is about deep belief in your goals, leading to positive actions.

You may have heard people say, 'Do what you love and you will succeed.' That is true because when you do something with passion, things happen fast. You often get growth, money and recognition. When you truly commit and love every part of your job, it's no longer work; it's your dream.

You got where you are with hard work. You are a designer who has talent and technical skills, but you also have the heart of an entrepreneur. There are two fundamental things in business: skill and mindset.

Most entrepreneurs have more than enough skill, but they lack the right mindset. Data suggests that

40–50% of small businesses fail within the first five years.[14] The owners of these businesses often don't need more skill to succeed; they need a better mindset. Over my years working with other business owners, I have found that 20% skill and 80% mindset is a strong ratio for success.

CASE STUDY: Changing a mindset, to change a business

Early on in my coaching career, I had a client who intrigued me. Let's call her Maria (not her real name). She was a talented designer who'd managed to get her brand off the ground on her own with no funding and turn it into a six-figure company. She was referred to me by another client of mine, so I was positive about taking her on. After all, she'd no doubt had long chats with her friend, so would know what to expect from our meetings.

I was surprised when Maria didn't jump into asking about marketing, profits, or employee issues; she just wanted to know why she was struggling so much, even though things seem to be going well. She was a pessimist who'd had many misfortunes over the years and she had trouble keeping up with the business growth. In fact, she wanted me to help her downsize because she was afraid she would fail.

I was sceptical about that and persuaded her to work with me on her reactions and mindset. She followed all the worksheets on reprogramming mindset that I use in my coaching while she worked on some business improvements. Within a month, she was good as new. She was now confident and positive, and she created healthy habits that benefited her business and her designs. She started working on new collections and grew her business sustainably to the level we'd agreed she'd feel comfortable with.

What is it that you truly want from life?

The best part about your brain is that it is a muscle. Just like your body, it can be trained and programmed to think, believe and succeed as you want it to; or you can let it drown in insecurity and anxiety. You control your reaction to events, and it's this reaction that gives you the outcome. Training your brain to focus on what it is you truly want from life takes commitment and self-belief, but it will differentiate you from those who go round in circles, trying to reach goal after goal, but never getting there.

It is time to stop blaming tax, competitors, the economy, or anything else you can't control and focus on what you can change, starting today. The difference between successful people and the rest is that successful people actively design their lives. The rest passively follow day to day with no aim or destination. They remind me of a conversation Alice had with the Cheshire Cat during her adventures in Wonderland:[15]

'Would you tell me, please, which way I ought to go from here?'
'That depends a good deal on where you want to get to,' said the cat.
'I don't much care where,' said Alice.

'Then it doesn't matter which way you go,'
said the cat.

Lose the procrastination

A common block to taking action and reaching your destination is procrastination. This is born from fears, habits, or excuses you tell yourself.

A few unhelpful excuses I hear from business owners wanting to avoid doing a task are:

- I always need to be in charge. I should be able to do whatever I want; it's my own business. I don't like boring tasks.

- Life is too short to waste any time doing what I don't enjoy. This task is too hard, too boring and no fun.

- I don't want to be a failure – what if I do it and fail? How will I face others?

- I'm not sure if I should – it is a risk. I won't do it if I am uncertain.

- I have low self-esteem – I am just not good enough.

- I am too tired, stressed, depressed or unmotivated.

Living by these excuses can lead to tasks piling up and problems staying unresolved. They also lead to lost opportunities and possibilities for your company.

Let's say you've had a long day and run out of time to complete your sales analysis report for the week. There are two possible routes you could take:

- **Route 1**. You get home and have dinner with your family → You feel too tired and tell yourself that it is Friday and you've worked hard all week → You decide to forget about the sales report and watch Netflix instead → You struggle to sleep because you are worried about how the business did that week → You decide to do the sales report on Monday → Come Monday, you are too busy and you end up going through another week stressed and unsure what your sales goal is as you haven't done the analysis on time.

- **Route 2**. You get home and have dinner with your family → You feel tired, but you tell yourself that although it is Friday, you will allocate thirty minutes to complete the report → You finish the report and watch a bit of Netflix → You sleep well because you know how the sales went and you are already thinking of next week's goals → You start your sales strongly on Monday because you know what you need to do → Your goal is clear and you can get your team to help you achieve it.

Changing our mindset can be very challenging as we all have a natural tendency to fall back into old habits. We all want to chill and do what others are doing, so we get sucked into everyday moments that drive us away from our goals. More stress, guilt, lack of achievement, depleted energy and low self-esteem follow as tasks pile up.

What is the alternative? To be extraordinary, you can't lead an ordinary life. You need to put in the hard work, starting by disciplining yourself to reject old habits. Small daily changes and decreases in procrastination will significantly pivot your achievements towards success.

Be your best friend – not your worst enemy

Imagine you could pick up a pen and write a chapter about your life, and this chapter would unfold and become reality. Would your chapter be about family? Wealth and business? Would it be about making a true impact on the world and eradicating poverty?

Think carefully. This chapter is not necessarily about business, although it could be. It is *your* chapter and you can make it exactly how you want it, but if business is a major part of your chapter, then it is a big part of you. It matters what you do with your business because it is in your life plan. Your ideal world. All you need now is to make it real.

Take a moment to think about your situation. Are you satisfied with your house? Your relationship? The amount of money you are making? Do you feel financially secure towards your future? If you have them, are your kids' financial future secure? Are you surrounded by the people who bring you joy? These are the types of questions to ask yourself while completing your life chapter.

There are few people in the world who are 100% satisfied with their life. Like most people, I want to improve and change certain aspects of my life and I will probably always find something to resolve, but this is only about the little things. I have mapped out the main aspects that truly matter to me and make a conscious decision every day to work on these, reflect on them and deliver.

The blame game

It is human nature to blame others. Often, we believe that our bad luck, action, or reaction is someone else's fault. It is our spouse's fault we are stuck at home with the kids; it is life's fault we don't make money because we come from a poor family (even though this is a difficult start, it has not stopped many well-known entrepreneurs from succeeding); it's our nanny's fault we can't get any work done because they're never on time.

Whatever the issue is, the truth is that there is a solution. You just need to find it.

A psychologist's research shows that between 70–80% of families are dysfunctional,[16] which begs the question: is the way you were raised compared to someone else a factor in your success or otherwise? Probably not. You have just as many chances to succeed as everyone else. The only one holding you back is yourself. You are the master of your own fate; no external relationships or circumstances can determine how successful or miserable your life will be. It will be what you make of it.

There are several things that tend to hold people back. Even when you know what they are for you, it doesn't make them any easier to overcome; if it was easy, everyone would be successful. Identifying if any of these resonate with you is a good place to start:

- You're following someone else's definition of success. That could be your partner's, your parents', friends', or a stranger's.

- Your mindset is not reflecting who you really want to be, in your industry or in your life in general.

- You are adhering to outdated norms and excuses: you didn't do well at college; you believe everyone is unhappy at work; that's life.

- You listen to everyone but yourself. Trying to please others then becomes your life goal.

- Fear of failure: your business is not performing, so this is the end.

- Believing money will solve all your problems. That's far from true. Money makes things a lot easier, but it's not the answer to success. A business that needs constant money investment will not be saved by a loan; it requires fundamental changes in structure and operation.

- You don't truly believe in yourself – you lack confidence.

For your business to grow, you need to achieve personal growth – and attitude is a big part of that. A belief that anyone's ability, intelligence or skill is set at birth is a common misunderstanding known as a fixed mindset. Psychologist Carol Dweck tells us that a fixed mindset leads to us being afraid to make mistakes because we feel it will give others a poor impression of us.[17] We see mistakes as a personal failure, when in fact, making mistakes and learning from them is the only way in which we grow. This creates a lack of personal growth and a tendency for us to avoid challenges as they might lead to failure.

The life of an entrepreneur is a life of risk taking. The more your business grows, the more employees you are responsible for. The more suppliers you work with, the more you can give back, but none of this can happen unless you take calculated strategic risks.

Dweck and her colleagues' puzzle experiments show how the mindset can truly change the way we approach life.[18] They did a series of experiments with children to study the effect of 'praise for effort' versus 'praise for intelligence'. All the children were given the same puzzle test and once they finished, half were praised for their effort and the other half for their intelligence. Then all were given a second test and after this test, they were praised again and asked if they would like the third puzzle to be an easier one or a harder one.

The results show that the children who were praised for their effort mostly chose to do a harder puzzle, whereas the children who were praised for their intelligence chose an easy puzzle. The fear of losing the intelligent label or even being questioned was too great to allow them to challenge themselves. They would rather be comfortably on the top of their game than risk losing their intelligent title.

As a child, you got what you got. It is too late to be raised any differently, but you can acknowledge your reaction to situations and understand your fears. That can be the key to escaping a vicious circle you might have been following for years.

Imposter syndrome

Some people suffer from imposter syndrome; in other words, they believe that they are not capable in their profession or that they are a fraud. True imposters never suffer from imposter syndrome. You are as capable as you allow yourself to be, and you know your business better than anyone. You are the only one who can know what you are truly capable of and it's your actions/reactions that will determine if that becomes a reality.

A struggle that many of my clients experience is a fixation on previous outcomes. For each entrepreneur who's arrived at a six- or seven-figure business, there were times when things weren't plain sailing. When old tricks don't yield the same results, for example, an ad campaign that is not performing as projected, there can be a cloud of confusion and desperation. This can create disappointment and a sense of failure.

Sticking with old tricks when the market is clearly shifting will only drain your cash flow and frustrate you. Your reaction will be what makes the difference. If you view change as an opportunity to learn, you can improve the result greatly. Build new strategies and new campaigns based on the latest data, not what's happened before.

The struggle of success

The old industrial age as we knew it is over. We have entered a digital era where the world is more connected than ever – dubbed Industry 4.0 or the Fourth Industrial Revolution. Those who have already jumped on that train are way ahead of the rest, but there are new challenges and new opportunities for us all. Instant gratification has become the norm and patience is a rare virtue as our society gratifies and indulges the need for speedy results. Long-term versus short-term thinking has been challenged.

When you post on social media, the algorithm will rate us. I'm sure we all know this. The results of each post, the time, the acceptance of the content, will be part of our code. We wait for our likes; within minutes, people are there showing us the love and we feel excited, happy, and satisfied.

Next time we post, we only get three likes. We feel disappointed and upset. Is it our visibility or our content that's at fault? Did our followers not like what they saw, or did they not even see it? Is it only the social acceptance we crave, or deep inside are we pleased when we get many likes as our reach won't be limited?

This rollercoaster of emotions is happening because we have set ourselves in the danger zone. We expect instant results, so we allow ourselves to be brought up and down by the traffic we get from social-media likes, website clicks, email open rates, etc.

Instant results are unrealistic

A generation or two back, people put true effort into their actions. They wrote long letters, had long conversations over the phone, travelled long distances to show others how they felt. They set their mind on a partner and committed to winning them over by being persistent.

Now we are experiencing a different world where we swipe right or left to accept or reject a potential partner based on a snap decision, and then we expect a date to turn into a marriage. It is understandable that the convenience of technology for everyday actions such as ordering food or watching our favourite show anytime we like has made parts of our lives easier, but it seems the whole world has lost the ability to be patient. Technology has not only shortened the distance between people, but as a result, it has shortened the time they are willing to wait to get or give a response.

'Good things come to those who wait,' my grandma used to say. I haven't heard anyone say that since. All I hear now is 'next-day delivery', 'click now, get it in two hours', 'no need to cook, get home-made meals to your doorstep', but if we treat the results of our business efforts like we view the likes on our social media, we are in for a big disappointment.

Your business needs strategy and clear vision of where it is going. To be the leader of the industry, to stand out in the crowd, you need patience and persistence. Sustainable growth can only occur when you stick to the process and pay it the right amount of attention in your market.

CASE STUDY: Finding my passion

When I graduated, I thought life would be easy. I'd gone to the top schools, finished a prestigious university and was ready to take over the world. Then due to personal reasons, I had to move out of London and things took an unexpected turn. I taught at university and got a job in my field. The university work was a great honour and I was proud to be teaching in such pre-eminent establishments, but something wasn't right for me.

After a few years, I realised that this was not what I wanted at all; it was what my family and everyone around me wanted me to do. They would say, 'But you are so good at it, why risk doing something else?' I knew I couldn't go on. My passion lay elsewhere.

Ironically, the family members who were so worried about my altered career path were the same ones who'd inspired it. One of the reasons I'm passionate about what I do is because I have been a designer and worked in design-related businesses my entire life. I grew up with parents who used design and business to entertain me and my brother. Some kids went to Disneyland; we went to every expo in Italy. My mother used to narrate the journeys of her past businesses instead of telling us fairy stories, highlighting alternative routes and analysing what and when things happened. My father would drag us to every site he was interested in developing and spend hours explaining his thoughts of how he would transform it with his vision. He always spoke of the client and how they would feel, rather than how much money the project would make him. Then he would take us to the construction site and explain why each rock and wooden beam was placed where it was and focus on every detail of the design. Their love and understanding of how business and design affect people's lives inspired me to enter this path in my own life.

I wanted to follow my passion and solve problems, designing and creating my own businesses. I wanted to have kids; I wanted my own house and to have the ability to make money, but I knew I had to make changes. I decided to move back to London and open my own business. Everyone was excited in the beginning. Despite their misgivings, my family was there for me, theoretically and physically, supporting, helping, advising in any way they could.

Then one mistake followed another: big investments; too many hours at work; common business issues. I didn't take a holiday in years. At that point, everyone in my family went back to questioning my decision.

'Is it all worth it?' my mother used to ask. 'Why don't you return to what you used to do? You loved teaching, didn't you? Maybe it's time to move on to another business.' A negative loop started in my life where I believed that perhaps I should just call it a day. At least everyone would get off my case.

At that stage, I was devastated. I was also very stressed. I became anxious and all I could think of was how to get rid of all my debt. My family had the best intentions, there is no doubt about that, but sometimes it is hard to hear your loved ones give up on your dream.

Then one morning, the answer came to me. I looked at my son, who was just a baby, and said, 'You are all that matters and I am actually super happy. You are healthy and you are smiling.' I smiled back at him and asked myself, 'How did I have it so easy with my work before when I wasn't even that interested in it?' The answer was simple: I believed to my core that I was on the top. No one knew better than me. My confidence and trust in myself and my knowledge gave me the strength to take actions to succeed in all I set my mind to.

I realised that this confidence is the key; that's what I was doing wrong. I knew exactly what I needed to do to make my new business profitable and I had all the tools.

I called my mother and told her that a business fails when you give up on it. I remember saying to her, 'I will not give up on mine because I know it can succeed.' She was proud; maybe she just knows me too well and knew her doubts would make me try harder.

I stopped occupying my mind with negative thoughts. My new path was a risk, but once my goal changed, everything began to unfold. A year later, all the business finances were sorted and the company was running to seven figures. The family norm was restored to phone calls filled with laughter and everyone minding their own business. I was happy and content with what I was doing, and I still am.

What scares you may hold the answer

It is hard to watch your loved ones struggle and it's human nature to try to remove them from what causes them pain. However, listening to others' opinions about you and your business, regardless of whether they're a family member or a colleague, can really bring you down.

When I shared my thoughts with my husband and we analysed why what people say bothers me so much, it was clear that I was scared of failure. Not so much failure in life, but failure in their eyes. That held me back and fed into my insecurity.

The truth is you can't control what people say. There are always people who will stand in your way, doubt you and remind you of mistakes you have made. The bottom line is what you believe, what you want from your life and what your mindset is. It's how you react, not how others act.

A common fear entrepreneurs face is having kids. They fear that kids will hold them back and ruin their work success. I have two kids and they haven't stopped me reaching my goals; they've motivated me to do better. When my boys ask for a story or playtime with me, I don't view it as a threat to my work. What is it all for if I can't spend time with my family? This is what it comes down to: balancing your priorities and finding a way to do everything that's important to you and do it well.

Remember that your business is not your life. It is its own entity. Like an organism, it exists in its own right. Its failure and success may reflect on you, but it does not determine who you are.

Everyone fails or succeeds at some point. It is what you do next – how you react – that determines who you are. Whether you believe you can achieve something or you believe you cannot, you will be right. We are the only ones who can know what we are capable of, and our actions/reactions will determine if that becomes a reality.

As an entrepreneur, you solve problems in the market and in your business itself. Your approach to your strategy and the way you build your business's ecosystem is what will give growth and success. This can only happen when you find what you're truly passionate about, your destination is clear and you direct your actions towards your goal.

ACTION STEPS

In this chapter, we have looked at how essential the right mindset is to the success of your business. You can have all the right skills, but without the mindset to complement them, you won't react to the external pressures of the business world and the internal stresses of running a business in the right way.

With the knowledge you now have, it is time to take action. Your next steps include:

- Download and complete the time analysis sheet, which you can find at: www.maakeacademy.com/designandgrow.

- Practise expressing what you want rather than what you don't want.
- Write a chapter of your ideal life.
- Write down five tasks/goals you would like to work on.
- Identify what holds you back and work on eliminating it.

5
Marketing

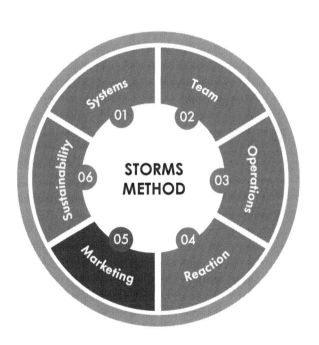

CHAPTER SUMMARY

The M in STORMS stands for marketing. There can be no business without marketing. Anything you do daily is about pitching your product, your vision, your story. The key to successful marketing is to focus on three aspects.

- **Leads** – you can't run a business without customers. Lead generation is one of the biggest parts of marketing.
- **Frequency** – by increasing the frequency of your customers' buying activity, you reduce the risk of them 'exiting' your brand, ultimately increasing their LTV (the average amount they spend during their lifespan as your customer).
- **Order value** – you need to upsell and increase your customers' order value, i.e., how much money they spend per order.

This chapter covers:

- The importance of knowing your market.
- How to clarify your niche and your avatar.
- Why you shouldn't try to sell to everyone.
- The perfect pitch.
- How to create funnels that convert.
- Effort doesn't mean results. How to take effective actions.
- How to increase your brand's visibility.

5

Marketing

This is the moment you have been waiting for! You've made it this far and now is the time to talk about increasing revenue.

Success in business cannot be achieved without money. It is the oxygen your company breathes. You need money when you start out and you need it to run your business. It is so essential that many entrepreneurs struggle to allocate it within their business and often make the mistake of economising on marketing.

What is the alternative? A business with no marketing is like a shop on the main street with covered windows or hidden in an alley with no signs or mention of it anywhere. To find it, customers would need to wander aimlessly, accidentally falling in through its door and having to guess what it sells. Clearly, this shop will have few to no customers.

Marketing is about solving the number-one problem that entrepreneurs face when launching or running a business: getting customers (this is called lead generation). Without leads, there is no business opportunity, no sales, no revenue and no profit.

A common question in the minds of businesspeople is, 'How much marketing is enough?' They ask marketing experts before they hire them; they ask their accountant how much of the budget they can spare; but one thing is for sure: no business can make money without spending (some) money.

For most brands, a minimum of 10–20% of their revenue should be spent on marketing. It is essential for the growth and sustainability of the business. Don't roll your eyes at that figure. Without investing in your vision, you are just waiting around for leads to fall into your lap, which is highly unlikely to happen.

Most entrepreneurs invest in marketing in one way or another. It can be as simple as wearing a T-shirt with your logo on or posting a picture of your product on social media, but some invest heavily in employing marketing agencies or freelancers. Sometimes, unfortunately, they have had negative experiences. Either way, the results can be confusing and the whole process can seem too complicated for many entrepreneurs to believe and invest in marketing. Have you experienced this?

Many brands are discouraged from marketing effectively due to the results they get initially. Results alone cannot define your marketing; there are many other parameters to investigate and many reasons for these results. The most important element of your marketing is your message. When your message is not clear, your marketing cannot bear fruit.

Effective marketing is based on strategy around funnels, visibility and the overall direction of your brand. The first step in your strategy is knowing who your ideal customer is.

Know who you are marketing to

Marketing has evolved over the years and the most drastic changes appeared when technology interfered in our everyday life. Newspaper ads and physical signs on the pavement have become online ads, notifications, and emails. They are no longer generalised, but highly targeted to a specific market. Monopoly of a product has become a distant dream, but the main core concepts remain.

CASE STUDY: Grandpa's market

My grandparents lived in a small village in the north of Greece. My grandpa had many jobs over the years. He travelled to Germany and worked in the mines, but the conditions were unbearable, so he decided to return to Greece and be a farmer.

He was a successful farmer, but his heart wasn't in it. He finally settled on something he loved doing, which was baking. Over the years, he transformed the front of the house into a fully functional bakery. The ground floor was full of machines: a massive mixer, big tables, and built-in ovens with black levers. My brother and

I had so much fun running around the ground floor trying to touch everything, until Grandpa chased us out.

The business plan was clear to him. It was a family business, and everyone would contribute. The goal wasn't to become rich; it was to have a comfortable life with his family and feed his village delicious fresh bread. His marketing was simple: he was the only bread baker in the village! He had the monopoly and if you wanted bread, his bakery was the place to get it. The alternative? Go over to the nearest town. There was no need for discounts, leaflets and a megaphone, because he had word of mouth. Everyone in the village knew he was the baker.

It could easily have stopped right there, but he was full of life and ideas. He decided to start selling my grandma's delicious vanilla cookies as well, offering them as a free sample in the beginning, and then upselling them. His market was small, and he had the advantage of knowing his customers. They were his friends, and he knew exactly who baked the most delicious cakes, so he started to partner up with them and used his shop to sell other people's goods.

Every morning when his customers arrived, he knew who would be needing what. He knew what time each one would show up. He truly knew his market.

As the business grew, it developed. People would call in and ask for favours, for example an order delivery because a parent or child was sick. This was the opportunity for him to hire a local kid with a bike and group his customers by proximity to the shop. He wanted to make sure the goods arrived hot, and he developed a system to achieve this.

Have you identified a few key principles from this case study? To provide great service, my grandpa made sure he knew exactly who his customer was. He understood his market and its pain points because his market was made up of his community and personal friends and he would ask them questions (much as business owners do with customer surveys). He might not have had CRM software, but he filled in forms with details of his customers, including what they liked and didn't like; what they and their families were allergic to. This information gave him a great advantage.

When the opportunity arose, he would create partnerships, upsell other products. He didn't need to buy the recipe for the product or even bake it; he just needed a partner who would do that. Most importantly, he evolved with the market's needs. When delivery was required and there was no partner, he hired help to expand his distribution and increase the convenience of his services.

Times have changed and now, gaining a monopoly is an unrealistic dream (unless you are the next tech genius). The good news is that you don't need to have a monopoly to be successful. The core of marketing is still the same; it's only the tools to deliver the message that have changed. The digital world has flooded the market with endless options for each product, so it often seems that the bigger a business is, the easier it is for it to be visible. That is true if you care about being visible to everyone, but unless you mass market, you'll be fighting a losing battle. What will pivot the scale is knowing who you want to be visible to: your ideal customer.

Your niche

What is a niche? Think of it as a small part of your wide market; a subcategory of the market you serve where your product aims to solve a specific need/problem.

When you first started your business, you picked something you love; something that means a lot to you and is aligned to your principles. Something that reflects who you are every day. You have taken time to perfect your product and build a brand around it that can be connected to the business's name, the packaging and copywriting as well as the product's general presence, both in social media and physically.

A common misconception in business is believing your product should be for everyone. Your brand exists because it solves a problem in *your* market, your niche, for your people. When your niche and your message are confusing to the market, the results will be confusing. Yes, you may have arrived where you are by focusing on a broad group of people. No one can take this away from you or from your brand, but what your brand may be missing is its target market.

Finding your niche can be challenging and sticking with it even more so. The fear of narrowing your reach is understandable as you don't want to leave money on the table. The problem is that without a clear strategy and audience, you will confuse your message. It will invite everyone and therefore no one to your doors.

Before the internet, finding your audience was a matter of location, location, location. The good news is that now the world has opened up, we are connected globally and there are endless possibilities. The market is evolving every day and new ways to be seen are being created.

At the same time, the algorithms of the big players like Facebook and Google have the power to change the game and stir up the market at any time. Stay informed by hiring experts to help keep you and your brand relevant while shining the spotlight on your market. For this to succeed, you need to be clear about who your market is and make decisions based on your niche.

Define your niche audience and concentrate on those people. You don't have to be married to your niche; you don't have to stick with it if you find that it isn't performing, but at the same time, you need to give it a real shot. Narrow it down, test it, iterate, and then make decisions based on results.

Leave your megaphone at home

I find it interesting how a lot of entrepreneurs I come across have the false belief that they are selling to everyone. Think for a moment of someone selling hotdogs. The hotdog stand is an example of mass marketing; almost anyone would potentially be willing to buy a hotdog – unless they are vegetarian/vegan and so on, in which case there are alternatives – but even though it seems to be a product for everyone, there are ways to increase its sales by focusing on a specific target market.

If you were planning to open a hotdog stand, you would consider its location and the time it would be operational. A stand that is open during lunch or dinner hours would do significantly better that a stand that works odd hours that are not related to mealtimes. The location plays a big part: the park might be quieter than a busy road next to offices, where the stand could make double the sales.

Even when the stand is doing well, it still has no niche or target audience. Its audience is random and the marketing strategy is 'please be hungry enough to buy one'. Right place, right time.

Say you know that X University has a crazy nightlife and everyone goes back to their dorms at 2am super hungry. What would happen if you targeted that audience? You could narrow your niche and even upsell. Now you have a stand at a specific location with a specific audience and you are going to sell the hotdog with a drink marketed as a deal. Your messaging can be bold and direct, aimed specifically at your niche, for example: 'Drink all night and still make it to class with our hangover cure.'

Now you are focusing on a niche market and your message is clear, the stand sales will significantly increase. On top of that, you will be upselling so your revenue will increase further as you are prompting each customer to spend more.

This simplified example shows you that the more specific you get with your marketing, the better results you can expect from less work than if you have the potential to appeal to everyone, but essentially market to no one. Another example could be a hairdresser. The technique used for cutting hair is generally the same. There are some small differences for men, women and kids, but most salons cover them all.

With kids especially, I find that the surroundings in the salon are important: a TV on, chocolate after the cut and a cool plastic vehicle they sit on and turn the steering wheel while they have their hair cut. Classic failure is when that steering wheel doesn't turn; then you have a very unhappy child who refuses to sit still.

CASE STUDY: Hair cut? No thanks!

One rainy morning, my husband and I took the kids to the hairdresser. At some point, my husband looked at himself in the mirror and decided that he really needed a haircut too. I looked at him and agreed. The hairdresser pointed out that she had a free spot after the kids' appointment, if he was interested.

He looked at her in shock. 'No, thank you,' he said. 'We have plans afterwards.'

When the boys were finished, we headed out. My husband looked at me and said, 'Can you believe her?'

I was a bit confused. 'Believe what? That she offered to cut your hair? You have a very similar trim to the boys and she did such a lovely job with their hair.' He stared at me and said nothing.

Why did he react this way? Although the hairdresser's cutting technique would have been the same for both my husband and our kids, we all lead our decisions with our emotions. We get a feeling about something, and then we rationalise it with our mind.

My husband probably found it ridiculous and unsettling to be offered a haircut with the kids' hairdresser; he may have worried she wouldn't have enough experience with grown-ups. Whatever the reason, he wanted to go to the hairdresser whose message is that they know what men need and specialise in cutting men's hair. This is the type of niche marketing that appeals to all of us.

A barber's shop in Manchester, which I've walked past a few times, always has a queue of men waiting outside – no woman in sight. The shop offers coffee and magazines and it's all about the beard. The owners truly understand their target market and customer. These men don't just go there to get their beard fixed; they go to enjoy the whole experience. It's a community and the stylists no doubt upsell all the related beard products successfully.

When you have selected your niche, you have certain advantages. You'll get your customers' attention without shouting through that megaphone; they'll feel as if you are reading their mind. You have their trust because you are solving their problem and you can get them to where they want to be, so your message needs to resonate with them. They need to feel that the action they are taking – choosing your brand – will solve their problem.

What about all the other potential customers, though? It is easy to think that getting out a megaphone to broadcast what your business is offering will attract more people to you, so more sales will occur. This will not happen and what's more, you need vast capital to invest to address everyone.

Mass marketing and branding work for big corporations because they serve a different kind of customer. Your business is not McDonald's, Apple or Amazon. If you really look into it, they also started with a niche market. Remember when Amazon only sold books?

You don't need everyone to know your name; you need your community and the right people to know who you are and what your product can do. That community will spread the word and more customers will come through your doors. Getting everyone's attention gets no one's attention. Your message will be lost, and you will be left unnoticed.

Get noticed by being a specialist and stop competing with everyone in your market. A bakery that makes cakes is competing with all bakeries. A bakery that does wedding cakes competes with all bakeries in the wedding cake industry. A bakery that does sugar-free organic cakes for weddings has a very specific target market.

Just to be clear – I don't mean you cannot offer a broad range of products or services, but you need to be strategic and mindful with separate campaigns for each category. Once you become king/queen of your niche, then you can pick another one and dominate it as well, but do it one at a time, not all at once.

It is to be expected that fear will creep in when you're focusing on a niche rather than a mass market; that happens to all of us. You don't have to cut business or stop serving others, but make a conscious decision that your strategy will focus on your ideal customer. Focus your resources and efforts on that goal. The speciality you offer and the price you are able to charge for it will be a lot more profitable than trying to be heard in a crowd.

Avatar

In your target market, there will be different types of people. Your avatar is your ideal customer: the description of one person in detail. The reason you create an avatar is to get into your customer's mind and emotions. How do they live their life? What are their worries, their desires, their dreams? Understanding their difficulties and their priorities can give you a clear path to effective marketing.

A common mistake is to create an avatar of who you wish your customer would be: the customer you wish you had. A large percentage of business owners I work with use their beliefs and values to create an imaginary character that ticks all the boxes. The issue with that is your customers might be buying your product for different reasons. They might care about the sustainable side of things, but care more about your colours and designs. They might be interested in the approach you have towards large clothing sizes or being inclusive rather than your trendy photos.

Whatever it is you believe your brand offers it needs to be confirmed with your market.

When you are creating your avatar, consider your customer's values, personality type and goals. You need to investigate the demographics and the psychographics. You need to identify their problems and how they deal with them. What would success and happiness mean to them?

You can achieve this through surveys and interviews. Speak to your clients and keep detailed notes about their lives and their situations. Do they mention kids, dogs, a walk at the beach? Any detail, no matter how small, can reveal a lot about their character.

Your ultimate goal is to solve your customer's problem. You can't do that unless you investigate what the symptoms are. You wouldn't accept a prescription from a doctor without a thorough examination, so using similar psychology, you can't expect people to buy your product if they don't believe you're qualified and knowledgeable about how to solve their particular problem.

The beauty of getting your avatar clear is that you are increasing your chances to create raving fans. These are customers who will buy at your price with no complaints, appreciate your product and recommend you or write a glowing review. They will stay with your brand and have a high LTV.

A business can have more than one avatar, and often they do. The process is the same; you just need different campaigns for different avatars. Your marketing must stay loyal to and concentrate on the details of who you are speaking to.

It's important to revisit your avatar as your business grows. You may wonder why this is. After all, by this point, surely you have your loyal customers and you're confident that you know what you are doing, right?

As your business grows, the demands grow with it. A small error or an oversight that might have been insignificant in the past can now become a tipping point for your revenue or even your business's survival.

I went to school in Switzerland. Although I have travelled a lot all over the world since then, the thing that has stayed with me is the Swiss people's incredible ability to put things in order. The trains are always on time; the streets are always clean; the people respect all the rules, even the unspoken ones. The feeling of calm in Geneva is unique in the world (at least to me).

It is no surprise that when an event or campaign goes without a hitch, we talk about it running 'like a Swiss watch'. The perfection of coordination, beauty and mechanism is a rare thing. Only the Swiss could have created such a product, because the attention to detail is in their culture and their blood. It's the way they are raised and view the world.

Run your business like a Swiss watch; only when all the gears are working together in perfect synchrony will the watch show accurate time and run smoothly. What would happen if you took that perfect watch and replaced a gear here and there with similar ones that are not quite right? The watch might still run, but seconds, minutes or hours might run late as it will no longer be able to reach perfect accuracy. The same will happen in business as small discrepancies can result in an increase to service bills and frustration levels.

That's how I view my business and every business I work with. Identifying the less-than-perfect cogs is the key to overall performance. Think of your avatar as one of the bigger cogs in your marketing strategy. You now know exactly the type of customer you are looking for and researching them takes on a lot more clarity. Nurturing these ideal customers rather than going after everyone is a clear strategy to achieving consistently predictable results.

Think of a beautiful garden filled with daisies and roses: a mixture of seasonal flowers that come and go, and long-lasting roses that will remain for years with the right care. Trying to maintain both types of flower can lead to some roses dying off. You water the daisies, but now they are surrounding your roses and restraining them from reaching their full potential. You become distracted and worried about too many flowers and end up not giving the right attention to any of them.

What if you made a conscious decision to care for only the roses? You actively remove the daisies or allow them to come to the end of their natural cycle without affecting your roses. By nurturing the roses, even though they are difficult flowers to tend, you can enjoy their blooms, which is something worth waiting for.

The right customers are worth nurturing and taking time with. Don't become distracted by small sales that are inconsistent, accidental or seasonal. Those are great, but they count as bonus sales, not as your predictable revenue.

Another advantage of a target market and a clear avatar is that they help with your pricing. When you are addressing a specific group of people and solving a specific problem for them, price can become unimportant to them.

Think of private healthcare. When you have a skin abnormality, for example, you don't run to the pathologist. You want to be seen by a dermatologist, and if you don't want to wait, you go private. Depending on your family history, you might go even further and find a private specialist in skin cancer. Either way, the price they charge becomes irrelevant if they can solve your problem. You don't lead your enquiry by asking about cost; you lead by asking how soon you can come in. In other words, you're asking how long you'll wait before you can give them as much money as they need to solve your problem.

Attract the right customers: the ones who can see your value and are willing to spend whatever it takes because they know you/your product will solve the specific problem they face. They know you want to change people's lives because that shows in the quality of your product or service and the care you take to deliver it.

Your number-one task with your avatar(s) is to find the gap between the current situation of your ideal customer and their desired situation. That is the solution you will provide.

Perfect pitch

I'm sure you've heard of the elevator pitch. In the movie *The Wolf of Wall Street*,[19] Leonardo DiCaprio's character uses a pen to demonstrate this. While he selects different people to pitch to him why he should buy the pen, everyone feels the time running out and that sense of urgency. He knows there is only so much time he can hold someone's attention, and therefore the pitch has to resonate with the problem and give a solution.

We live in a world where no one wants to spare any time. Time has become the most valuable asset in everyone's life and it's traded very carefully. Rehearsing your pitch and perfecting it is not only important for you and your team to get the sale; it is also part of showing respect for other people's time, and that's not all. Choosing the right time to pitch is as important as delivering a perfect pitch. People are occupied with their own life and intruding into that life, no matter how beneficial your product or business might be to them, will not be welcomed.

Approaching someone while they are having dinner at a restaurant with their family and pitching will be a disaster. Booking an appointment with someone so they will have your full attention is ideal. Pick the right times and ensure that the recipient is not interrupted or ambushed by your presence.

When you are in a meeting, whether it be with a potential client or other businesspeople who may become partners, you can quickly separate the newbies from the professionals. You know which client has researched the market and who has chosen you from the top three to five brands in your market, who came across you because you were recommended and who found you by accident.

Remember that potential customers most likely know who you are, if you are a leader in your industry, your pitch should be clear and your knowledge should be reflected in your professional approach. You form an opinion of others, and they form an opinion of you. While you are assessing if they can be an ideal customer, they are assessing if you are the right person for them to pay their money to get the result they want.

The pitch is your most powerful tool to identify who you are. It should include all the information a potential customer or business partner needs to decide whether it's a good investment of their time to take this relationship further.

The most important element of all pitches is to be clear, consistent and engaging. Working on your pitch brings a lot of value to your business. It gives clarity and confidence, both to you as the founder and to your team. Unified, your brand can pitch consistently and powerfully.

Creating digital funnels that get conversions

You have your niche, your message, and your perfect pitch. Now you are ready to put it all into action.

All your customers pass through funnels. A digital funnel is the journey they take from being introduced to your company until they decide to buy or exit. The exit part is the interesting one because you are in control of how soon that will happen.

It depends on your customer's state of awareness. They could be problem unaware, problem aware or ready to buy. You lead each customer to a different funnel depending on your marketing strategy and their state. There are many marketing tactics to move potential customers from one state of awareness or one phase of the lead generation funnel to the next, including content pages, webinars, and sign-ups.

The beauty of funnels is that they are full of data. When you have data and results that you can measure, you no longer live in a land of hope and uncertainty; you can predict what will happen with accuracy. The data also allows you and your team to observe the performance of your marketing strategy, iterating and trying again if necessary. The only true judge of your marketing efforts is the market itself, so set your goals clearly and follow through with conscious decisions. A strategically created funnel builds mutual trust and open conversations and gets results.

Advertising campaigns

In marketing, you will need to launch many campaigns and experiment with them daily, weekly and monthly to get optimal results. When your background is in design, pattern making or anything other than marketing, it is nearly impossible to embrace this part of the business. This is where it's important to hire the right team of experts.

Knowing what you want to get out of each campaign can be the difference between successful marketing and money wasted. There's so much information and there are so many avenues to pursue in this area, it's easy to get lost and confused about your priorities, but the bottom line is simple.

You need to generate new leads. You also need to encourage frequency of repeat orders from your existing leads, along with a high order value (the amount the customer will spend on each order). Simple, right?

Just because it's simple doesn't mean it's easy. To get all that, you need to take many steps.

When your aim is to increase leads, concentrate on lead generation funnels. Create several campaigns and have a clear goal of what you expect each one to achieve. To create leads, you need to invest in paid and organic advertising content. There are pros and cons to each option, but for strong marketing, you need both organic and paid-for traffic.

Organic content is free to publish, and therefore has a great return on investment (ROI). There is the cost of the time it takes to generate the content by yourself or the cost of paying for a copywriter as well as the software and tools you use, but it is a long-term investment as it can keep generating leads with no time limit once it's created. If done correctly, organic advertising content leads to web presence and brand awareness. It is ideal for your target audience because it is educational and keeps giving them relevant value. The customer is likely to view your brand as a source of education on how to solve their problem. You can provide them with this education through blogs or videos.

The key to organic content is to think it through. If you are looking to capture new leads, give them opportunities to download something of value. If you are looking for conversion, lead visitors to specific pages on your website. Don't put content out there that doesn't have a funnel or a strategic reason to exist.

There are a few caveats about organic traffic. For one, it takes months/years to build, especially if you are not using experts. Your content must reach the top three to five results on internet searches to be in the game, so you need expertise and in-depth knowledge in several areas.

Organic traffic is slow and hard to scale, but don't get disheartened. There is hope in the form of software and tools that can help. SEMrush and PageOptimizer Pro are popular software with strong keyword tools. You might also have come across some SEO help in WordPress. For updated tools and software visit www.maakeacademy.com/designandgrow.

Unlike organic traffic, paid-for traffic has instant results. You are in control of your budget and can spend as much or as little as you wish, but as soon as you stop paying, your ads, and therefore your reach, stop. You can track ads in real time and see your results instantly, along with data you can analyse to understand why the campaigns work or not.

You are no longer restricted by the old marketing techniques like ads in newspapers that you hoped your audience would get a glimpse of. You can now be as selective as you wish. You can filter and choose your target market based on interest, activity and many other attributes, but whoever runs your ad campaigns needs to know what they are doing and be methodical.

Paid ads are extremely competitive and the price can fluctuate depending on the market or season. The harshest thing to stomach is that you get penalised. An example of this can happen if your ads are set for conversations and your website does not convert a lead to a paying customer. One penalty can be that your next ad might be shown to less people or the price of each click on your ad might increase. With that in mind, assess the needs of your business and allocate money according to the stage it is in and what your goals are.

An important thing to know is how aware your customers are. Most customers are not ready to buy. They might not even be aware of their problem or they could be in denial. They might simply not be able to afford your product yet, but the most common reason they aren't ready to buy is that they just don't know enough about your product or company, and they won't blindly trust it.

The mind is trained to seek security and trust, especially when we're in need of or desire something. Let's assume you are craving something sweet like chocolate and you share your thoughts with me. When I ask you what type of chocolate you would like without providing you with choices, you will most likely choose your favourite as you will recall the feeling of enjoyment you had the last time you ate it. Rarely will anyone answer, 'I would like to try a new brand, please.'

In a similar vein, when a customer comes across your product, possibly for the first or even the second time, they might need a bit of convincing that it is worth taking a risk on. Taking a risk on something new requires good timing. That's why nurturing your leads has such high conversion rates.

Only 3% of your customers will be ready to buy from you.[20] That leaves 97% of customers who won't want to buy at first sight. Those are the ones you want to nurture. Let's say nurturing leads to 35% of those customers becoming interested in buying from you now or in the future. That's a big increase on your conversion rate; just by nurturing, you can add another 35% to the 3% of customers who convert immediately. That 38% would make a big difference to your ad budget and overall revenue.

There is no denying that in a digital world full of endless information, nurturing a customer and allowing them to mature in their decision making is the most effective way to ensure a ROI. Marketing automation for nurturing prospects is a large growth sector, with users seeing a large increase in sales and productivity whilst reducing their marketing overheads.[21] Companies are waking up to this, finding innovative new ways to autonomously connect with their customers, in a personal and meaningful way.

New leads versus existing customers

A common mistake I come across is the level of importance business owners put on new leads. They have strong branding and run expensive campaigns with one aim alone – gaining new leads. It's as if the number of leads is the only thing that matters.

New leads alone cannot generate growth. Each new lead has an acquisition cost: the total amount of money you spend on acquiring the customer (marketing cost + sales cost) in a set period of time divided by the number of new customers acquired. Constantly generating new leads without nurturing them can prove very expensive as you have to pay the acquisition cost again and again.

This is where the lifetime value (LTV) of the customer comes in. When a customer keeps returning to your brand, you have no more acquisition costs for that customer and your profit on the second, third and so on sale will be much higher than on the first order of a new customer.

Of course, new leads are necessary. Always seek your ideal customer and have a strategy of how many you are after. At the same time, don't allow your lead generation to distract you from your existing customer list, which is like a hidden treasure. It's a mixture of your regular return customers, occasional ones, customers who no longer buy and leads who have never been converted. These non-converted leads were created from your funnels and your marketing efforts and cost money. You managed to get their attention for a reason, so nurture them. Otherwise, you are missing an opportunity to get a ROI from them. At the same time, your existing customers will be slipping away if you're not nurturing them too.

Ideally, you want to utilise your existing customer list and take steps to reactivate leads who have been inactive for a while. Depending on your product, you'll find your customer's buying cycle will vary. It is important to know your ideal customer's buying cycle, but as a rule of thumb, most brands work with a ninety-day window. After that, they consider the customer lost.

How to nurture your customers

There are many ways to approach a list of existing active and inactive leads. You can use automated emails, snail mail or calls, but the aim is always to remind the customer why they showed interest in or purchased your product in the first place. You could send a simple card, a discount code or, even better, a brochure with your products explained in it.

Personalise the mail if possible. In a world that moves so quickly, people are busy, forgetful and have far too much to deal with. You need to stand out and make the customer notice you. If you use snail mail, use a fun-coloured envelope and handwrite the card inside. If you use email, then make it stand out and ensure it's personalised to your customer as much as possible.

For nurturing via telephone, get your team to call as many customers as possible from the list.

Have one team member start with the customers who haven't bought in over ninety days and another call those reaching sixty days. On average, a salesperson can reach fifty to sixty customers a day via phone calls, with a maximum of eighty to 100 calls to get the best results. These leads are the low hanging fruit, so aim to convert 10–20% to get them back in the game.

There are company owners who can't afford to have salespeople on the phone all day or feel that these calls intrude on the customer's life too much. Make sure your team approaches the calls by showing interest in how the customer can improve their life and how your product can help. Perhaps do some research on what they are working on and suggest a related new product they might be interested in.

Another technique that works well is to create demand. Instead of calling, send an email offering a limited time for customers to reach you. Have your calendar available; www.calendly.com has excellent and easy ways to incorporate your work calendar so you are never double booked. This way you get the clients to commit to talking with you rather than spending your day calling around and interrupting their day while making yours less productive.

Email marketing

Whether they're on your new or existing leads list, your customers need nurturing. On top of snail mail, calls and other tactics that you use, the most effective and consistent way to nurture your customers is through email marketing.

Email marketing is a major part of e-commerce, and yet many small and medium businesses overlook it. A person spends more than 3.1 hours daily on emails, according to an Adobe survey.[22] In five working days that adds up to 15.5 hours per week. In a calendar year of fifty-two weeks, we now have 806 hours on emails alone or twenty weeks in a year. Is that you? I probably spend more, but I have come across entrepreneurs who hire staff just to get their email inbox filtered. It might sound extreme, but if you think about it, time is precious, and you need to determine where it is best allocated.

When you invest in email marketing for your business, you need to commit to it. Email marketing software and CRMs have made it easier than ever to filter and segment customer lists as well as create automation, giving endless opportunities to approach the right customers with the right message at the right time.

There are many types of software you can choose from for email marketing. I would avoid Mailchimp as your company needs a more sophisticated and complex tool at this stage. I find Klaviyo to be a strong tool with increasing possibilities, but there are plenty more that can deliver what you need. See updates and tool suggestions on www.maakeacademy.com/designandgrow.

You can use the analytics of your chosen software to see the results of your campaign. There will be information on email open rates, email clicked rates, placed orders, placed order value and more. CRMs like HubSpot even have data on if/when emails are opened and by whom. This is a good start to track how your email campaigns are doing and understand how well your content has been received by your audience.

As with any tool, this software must be used correctly. Inexperienced marketers often use sporadic, randomised mailing without strategy. They don't analyse the data and leave the business with confusing results.

That's money left on the table; let me explain why. Using email marketing and automatic email sequences (flows), a series of prewritten emails that are automatically scheduled to be delivered to specific customers/subscribers upon their online actions, increases customer activity and LTV. You might be using the odd email broadcast here and there when you have an offer or when you are running low on cash, but that's the tip of the iceberg with email marketing. Yes, people are tired of their inbox getting full, but they do filter what they don't want out and keep the special few, and they commit to reading that content. You need to become one of the few by using strong headlines and valuable, educational content.

There are five non-negotiable email flows that all brands need:

- Welcome series flow

- Post-purchase nurture flow

- Abandoned-cart flow

- Cross-sell flow

- Browse abandonment flow

There are many more, but the bottom line is that you need to be segmenting your existing list as well as creating flows for new leads.

On top of your flows, which are a key automation in your marketing, you also need to create broadcasts. These are manually set emails containing details of your latest news, products and offers, which will go to your customer list when scheduled.

Consistency beats originality – don't delay by looking for the perfect topic or edit the same email hundreds of times. Get your team ready to start with one broadcast email a week, if you don't do this already, then move to two a week. You can go up to five a week, but personally I think three is enough for your product and brand to stay in people's minds. Any more can become irritating and cause customers to unsubscribe from your list.

Ideally, 20–30% of your emails need to be educational. If you send twelve emails a month, make three to four educational. The more you increase your educational value, the more engaged your customers will be. Yes, writing valuable content is time consuming; it requires effort and copywriters can be expensive. All that is true. This is why you need to analyse your lists and clear out all the customers who are not engaging. Your team has to resend campaigns to those who don't open the email the first time and they can do this by recycling content from years or months ago, saving you some of that precious time.

Another use of the broadcast email is to encourage testimonials. Everyone knows that ads portray the best version of your brand and you would say anything to sell your product, so customers turn to reviews on Google, Trustpilot, your website or email testimonials. They want to know what others are saying about your product, not what you are saying as a brand, so have your team encourage reviews, testimonials and tagging. If you can get your hands on them, video testimonials are the most effective. Once you start getting those, pat yourself on the back because you have done well!

How to increase your brand visibility

People connect to people, to their stories. They are curious about who you are and why are you doing what you are doing. Customers want to know why they should trust you or your brand.

I remember years ago, a couple were looking for funding for a kid's non-spill cup. They explained how their product started strongly, how their own child inspired them and so on, but then the woman got very sick and the couple couldn't keep up with the business, so sales slowed down.

Yes, it is rather reminiscent of American daytime TV, putting people's personal struggles on display for better ratings, but the truth is that I remember the story, particularly the mother's story, and not because I felt sorry for her. This woman had a mission and vision, and she didn't give up. She believed in her product; her passion and her story were what made me check out her brand. It wasn't only about the product anymore; it was about her story. The way she described why she wanted to create that product because her child used to spill water everywhere. There are many non-spill cups on the market, but this one had a friendly, approachable face that gave me something more than perfect product pictures.

Social media

Many people are reluctant to be part of the online social scene. I was like that for years, too; I needed a little push to show me that sharing my story and engaging my customers is more important than ever.

I am not talking about sharing pictures of your dinner or you walking your dog; I am talking about your business and personal online presence. Online platforms such as Facebook have settings that allow you to protect your personal life and share posts only with selected groups. You might want some aspects of your life to be shared exclusively with friends and family and have others that can be seen by everyone. As you become more visible through your brand, customers might become curious and want to follow your personal story. Use your personal social media as well as your business social media to post business-related material and share stories that speak to your ideal customers.

Choose the social media your customers like to use. Fashion and interior designers are often found on Instagram and Pinterest as those platforms are great for visibility and sales. A brand is judged by its number of followers, so an online social media presence is essential.

Be consistent and professional in the use of your branding. Think of your avatar and post relevant content to solve your customer's problem. Social media is a great place for your messaging to attract the right customers.

Become an industry leader

Another way to be visible is to become an industry leader. You can be the one to attract customers through the valuable content you post via your personal social media accounts, your podcasts and your lectures.

Being an industry leader is a powerful way to stand out in the crowd as you present yourself as the expert, but it doesn't happen overnight. You need consistent and valuable content, but even if it takes you years to establish yourself as a leader in your industry, it will still be worth it. Start today. Take action and plan content creation into your week. Post videos, get involved with the industry-related press and make your mark.

Partnerships

Want another way to get visible? Use the power of the market by investigating how partnerships can help launch your brand into the spotlight. Nespresso was struggling to get attention, until it partnered with George Clooney. Suddenly, everyone wanted that coffee machine in their home. It was the new trend. The idea is that everyone wants to be glamorous like George Clooney, creating an attraction to the product.

Nespresso has also used influencers such as Chiara Ferragni, whom maake has also partnered with in the past, marketing a cup with her name on it and using her 27.7 million followers to reach Millennials.[23] These partnerships are all well-strategised moves that aim to improve the brand's profile and, more importantly, its revenue.

The objective of partnerships can be broken down into three sections. The way I approach it in my coaching business is to help brands get RID (raise, improve, distribute) of invisibility. These three sections help your brand succeed, and you should already have covered two of them.

This is the way I explain it to my staff when we use RID in our business. **Raise** is about having a strong appearance in the market (an established name), **improve** is about having a strong product, including how the market views the product, and **distribute** is about the means you have to send it out and the reach you have. Covering only one aspect would make you a good candidate for someone else to partner with; two out of three would give you the grounds to propose a strong partnership with a high-profile third party.

You know what you are missing and what you want to achieve. If you are looking to raise your brand's profile, you could partner with a strong name (celebrity, influencer or another brand). If your brand is already an established name, but you need help to improve your product or technical expertise, you could partner with someone who has the latest tech or the means to refine your product or add something to your range. If you want to add to your distribution channels and expand your reach, then focus on partnering with others who already have the customer reach.

Are you still with me? Take a big breath; it's a lot to take in, but the thing to remember is that you are not alone. You have your team. Hardly any of the marketing tasks we've covered need to be done by you. This is about you getting your house in order, so to speak.

ACTION STEPS

In this chapter, we have covered the importance of your marketing campaigns. You need to be aware of where each customer is in your sales funnel and target them with the correct material to nurture every one of them.

Now it's your time for action, including:

- Define your niche.
- Create your avatar(s).
- Perfect your pitch.
- Review marketing KPIs.

- Nurture all your customers; don't just concentrate on new leads. You will get a far better ROI from returning customers.
- Reactivate your existing customer list.
- Set up email flows.
- Schedule your email broadcasts.
- Become more active on social media with valuable content.
- Create even more valuable content to become a leader in your industry. This may take years to achieve, but it will be worth it.
- Consider partnerships with those who can raise, improve or distribute your product, getting RID of invisibility.
- Find updates and tool suggestions for automating your advertising campaigns on www.maakeacademy.com/designandgrow.

6
Sustainability

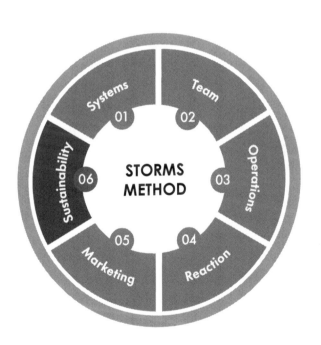

CHAPTER SUMMARY

The second S in STORMS stands for sustainability. The aim of this chapter is not to put you on the spot; it's to open up the box of possibilities and small changes that can help shape a better future. You and your company can make a difference.

This chapter covers:

- What your social responsibility is and how you can become more sustainable in your business.
- Fast and slow fashion – the vision of printing on demand.
- The accountability of the supply chain and how to source responsible suppliers.
- The basics of textile certification.
- An introduction to organic cotton and recycled polyester.
- How your brand can take action in your premises, packaging and message.
- Giving back without breaking the bank.

6

Sustainability

Over many years, the world has become polluted through the selfish ways of humankind and the results are affecting us all. Luckily, the vast amount of information, along with charities and world leaders coming together, has pivoted the attitude of society. The world has become more responsive and more responsible, and businesses are actively joining the fight against pollution and climate change.

In business and in life, there is strength in a team that moves towards a common vision. United Nations member states got together in 2015 and devised seventeen sustainable development goals (SDGs).[24] World leaders with a vision set high goals to deal with climate crisis, hunger, human rights, extreme poverty and more, starting a marathon to get the word out and enable people to join in their mission. Famous actors, musicians and other leaders have done so and helped spread the word, and this is still ongoing. This mission is an honourable one and any business or individual that joins is committing to a better tomorrow.

Our social responsibility

As an entrepreneur, you have a desire to stand out in the crowd. You want to succeed, to get noticed, but if your vision doesn't include giving back to the world and being a force of true change, your journey might not shine as brightly as it could.

You have a responsibility to yourself, your family, your employees, your customers and the world. When you think of responsibility, think on a big scale, then bigger and even bigger. Think of you and every business, every individual working together to be part of a more sustainable world.

You're possibly tired with people pushing on about becoming more sustainable and helping the world. Maybe you've heard this all before and wish you could help, but your business is not profitable enough. You may even donate some money from time to time, thinking that you will revisit this and increase your donation when the time is right for more consistent action. I am as guilty as any of thinking this way.

I used to believe that there would be a right time one day, but not today. Then I looked around the factory and saw fabric being chucked into the bins. Good fabric that was usable but was an overrun from the production process or it hadn't passed our colour quality control, maybe had a minor fault. There might have been an error on the design, but the fabric itself was in excellent condition. That fabric could have been used to make blankets for the homeless or clothes for a charity shop. It could have been reused on many projects; it just wasn't suitable for sale.

After going into a deep dive, I realised that fabric waste is a much bigger issue than I'd thought. In the UK, approximately 200,000 tonnes of textile waste are produced each year.[25] Studies have shown that every person in the UK produces 3.1 kg of this waste. From that, only 0.3 kg is recycled, and 0.4 kg is reused.[26] Thanks to fast fashion (more on this later in this section), 1.7 kg of fashion clothing waste per person per year ends up in landfills.[27]

How can the UK textile industry become more environmentally friendly?

There is no excuse for throwing so much fabric away. I realised something had to be done and my business had to play its part, but after long searches, Alexander and I had found few organisations that deal directly with this matter.

The UK's Sustainable Clothing Action Plan (SCAP), which has been in place since 2020, is worth paying attention to.[28] Created by those in the industry, including fashion brands and retailers, fabric manufacturers and textile recyclers, SCAP has a policy to reduce the impact of waste in fashion clothing in the UK. The way its creators believe this can be achieved is by introducing new, more sustainable textiles to the fashion market.

This organisation has spent the past two years doing valuable work to contribute to the SDGs. It's convened various workshops and groups, set targets, measured and calculated progress; it has also shared expertise so that a vast proportion of the UK textile industry can reduce the carbon, water pollution and waste impacts of fashion clothing products.

CASE STUDY: maakeLess fabric waste

As textile manufacturers and printers, my team and I are working towards creating circular economy action – we believe that reusing and recycling textiles can help our economy grow. These efforts reduce the impact of our industry on nature and climate change and assist people to lead sustainable, healthy lives. This is why we strongly advocate reusing the textiles that we manufacture.

This is how maakeLess fabric waste was born. We have a clear mission to reduce fabric waste from manufacturing facilities and do our best to give fabric a second life. Starting with small calls and emails, we sent fabric to schools for art projects, crafts and use in plays; to fashion universities, designers, and craft centres; in fact, to anyone who could find a use for it. Seeing these people excited and engaged made all the difference to us as it confirmed that designers and clothes manufacturers are in this together. We're united to build a better future.

Becoming more sustainable

You might wonder how this is directly related to your business. Every entrepreneur must make choices about their production, suppliers and how they deliver the final product. How they give back. Being sustainable is not just about fixing what's broken; it is also about preventing the problem as much as possible.

A good place to start is with your premises. Think of all the resources you use daily and how those can be altered to create a more sustainable outcome. The amount of energy and water you use can be two easy fixes. By changing your provider or implementing stricter rules around the use of these resources, you immediately make your premises more environmentally friendly.

Then comes your product. Consider the material you use and the techniques and methods available and at your disposal in the industry. You can review and optimise each one and reduce their impact on the world. For example, poorly designed patterns can create unnecessary waste. Old sewing machines can use double the energy of modern ones and collections that you don't sample first can result in hundreds of metres of faulty product that cannot be used.

Pattern making is an art in itself and there are designers who are truly committed to delivering a minimal waste product. Several brands such as Malaika New York, Ecoalf, Zero Waste Daniel and Tonlé use this as part of their mission statement and have structured their brands around it. They make it well-known, create content and spread the word every chance they get.

Your business may not be positioned for such extreme branding, but don't let this stop you from having a stand on this matter. Align your message, make your values visible on all platforms and, most importantly, work on your product creation to achieve your desired result, mindful of your waste.

Designers are no strangers to problem-solving and inspiration comes in the most unexpected ways. Organising your patterns efficiently can reduce waste significantly as small design changes can improve the pattern and the result. Cut-offs can be reused in product bags, purses, hats and other accessories that can be included in the delivery of your product as a gift or sold separately.

When you print on fabric digitally, the method and the ink you use will deliver a variety of colour strengths. The question is, do your brand values align with using a product that is so heavy on water, waste and resources compared to a much more sustainable technique? You may be surprised by the number of people who call in or send samples to digital printing factories to complain that the print is not a match to another fabric print.

Brands that are ignorant about printing methods believe that print is print as they do not understand the process. It is your responsibility to make an informed decision as an entrepreneur, designer and human being. This is your opportunity to take action. Ask your supplier questions and find out how your product is made. Be informed on what this means to the world, to your customers. You might choose less sustainable methods and that is your decision to make but make it knowingly.

Fast fashion

'Did you see that dress on the Parisian catwalk last week?' you ask your team. Then days later, you see similar dresses pop up on Instagram. Social media influencers getting attention from the world have created the need for fast fashion.

In research done on the United States so-called fast fashion formula, McKinsey stated that a person buys a new piece of clothing approximately every five days.[29] In a year, that amounts to approximately seventy-three outfits. Compare that to the 1980s, when reports show that the average American bought fewer than fifteen items of clothing a year.[30] Their spending activity on clothing now comes up at approximately 10% of their income and they're buying five times the amount they used to buy.

Where are all the classic garments made with high-quality skills and well-thought-out patterns? They have been replaced with rushed work on cheap fabrics to catch the trend; to be affordable for that Instagram post, and then discarded. This shopping attitude has been feeding the industry messages of urgency, low pricing and speedy delivery, and shipping these goods across the world invariably has an effect and impact on carbon emissions.

According to the Carbon Literacy Project, in 2021, the fashion industry was the second-largest industrial polluter, accounting for 10% of global pollution and 20% of waste water.[31] Research by the UN Climate Change team has predicted that with the rapid increase in production in the past twenty years, if it continues at this rate, fashion could account for more than a quarter of all global carbon emissions by 2050.[32]

Accountability of the supply chain

When was the last time you visited an overseas mill to see its production and the conditions its employees work under? How recently have you checked where its waste effluent is going? Its managers might tell you it is all safe and done correctly, but do you believe them?

Why does this matter? Surely these mills just print for you and you get your fabric at the price you need to make a profit.

Accountability of the supply chain is becoming more and more important, especially for consumers. You might remember major incidents such as the collapse of the Primark Rana Plaza factory in Bangladesh.[33] These incidents were met with swift condemnation from the global community, with the Pope speaking of 'Living on 38 euros a month'[34] and a *Harvard Business Review* report showing that consumers have more power than they think when it comes to making choices about where they shop.[35]

Consumers are using this power. According to research by Oeko-Tex in 2019, 69% of Millennials say they investigate claims of sustainability and eco-friendliness when they research clothing purchases.[36] Customers care more about provenance and demand more transparency about supply chains than ever before. They not only look for how the items are made and what materials they are made from, they increasingly search for how ethical and sustainable the brand is. How the brand values align with their own personal goals and feelings.

It came as no surprise that the UK Fashion and Textiles Association (UKFT) found that the three biggest opportunities facing the industry in 2021 were compliance towards sustainability (encompassing waste reduction, resource efficiency, energy use and responsible sourcing), social media and buying locally online.[37] Furthermore, it found trade policy to be one of the largest challenges.

Customers are using social-media platforms to promote sustainable fashion brands, with a growing movement towards locally produced items made from dead stock or made to order. With the growth of Depop, ASOS Marketplace and Instagram Shopping, local brands have a greater ability to reach customers and interact with them in a way that bigger brands cannot.

The good news is that the industry is waking up to this and people are seeing the benefits of moving production back to the UK. This doesn't just go for small businesses; corporations are also seeing the benefits of manufacturing close to the final market.

Is this right for your business? What would you say if I told you that you could build a sustainable business model where you could deliver to your customers in less than a week and not hold any stock? Where you only pay for what you use and order what you need? What if I told you that this could all be done in the UK by staff paid a living wage, using Oeko-Tex-approved inks and fabrics (tested for **harmful substances**), in a water-free sustainable manner by a mill using 100% renewable electricity? This can all be done for a similar price to buying abroad, with catwalk-quality printing and superb CS that responds in minutes, not days, in a language you understand.

At maake, a leader in textile printing and manufacturing in the UK, this is done daily with a shared vision to make a world where people order only the fabrics they need and they are produced just for them, when they need them.

The rapid growth of 'slow fashion' has driven the need for localised production to make its business model work – a model based around producing only what is ordered. Slow fashion is the epitome of 'pull' production, utilising a just-in-time methodology where you get the order from your customer first, then you place orders with suppliers. Customers will usually accept a longer lead time, knowing that items are specifically made for them.

The vast majority of brands use this method now for various reasons. For example, micro businesses use it as a way to control their costs by only producing whatever they need.

Textile certification

Your choice of fabric will play a vital role in your product's success. Textile certifications help brands understand how sustainable and safe each fabric is. Every respectable brand should be aware of the terminology and its importance to each fabric.

You have a responsibility as an entrepreneur to ensure your final product meets certain requirements before it is sent out into the market. These include standards and regulations that are applied to the industry as well as certifications that refer to the sustainability of a product.

You have likely come across the two most important certifications on your own fabrics in the small text on labels. One is the Global Organic Textile Standard (GOTS), a certification that ensures the organic status of textiles from the moment the raw material is harvested, all the way through the manufacturing processes to the final product. The other is Oeko-Tex, which was created by a group of seventeen independent research and test institutes throughout Europe and Japan that focus on the textile and leather industries, testing for harmful substances and to promote customer confidence and high product safety. They support the SDGs.

When you vet suppliers and pick your fabrics, make sure you understand what you are buying. You need to feel confident that you have all the information required to make an informed decision. This is why I am including a standard list of certifications for easy reference.

BS5867

If you want to reduce the fire risk of your curtain products, you need to use those that are certified by BS5867 Part 2, Type B and C standards.

Crib 5

This is a rigorous test for upholstery fabrics. When they pass the Crib 5 test, they are issued with the code: BS 5852:2006. This means that they meet UK fire regulations and are classed as Crib 5 compliant.

For furniture to meet this particular standard, it has to pass three tests which are designed to specifically prevent the outbreak of fire in everyday life:

- **Test one: the smouldering cigarette test.** (BS EN 5971) A cigarette is left to burn for its whole length within a crevice, made from the fabric and a frame. The fabric must not catch alight or smoulder if it is to pass the test.

- **Test two: the match test.** (BS EN 5972) The match test is similar to the above test but involves a burning match.

Only once the material has passed the first two tests successfully can it continue to the third and most important test, the Crib 5. If it fails one of the first two tests, it cannot go any further in the certification process. The Crib 5 test employs a small wooden structure made up of wooden planks, five tiers high with the fabric, and must resist ignition and smouldering for ten minutes.

EN71-3

Predominantly used for toys, EN71-3 standards indicate that a sample of a particular fabric has been tested independently to make sure it contains no or trace amounts of certain chemical elements and heavy metals. The EN71–3 certificate shows that the fabric is safe according to European standards.

Flame retardant for upholstery

There are three main ways that upholstery fabric may become fire retardant. Firstly, the fabric may consist of and be woven from yarns which are inherently fire retardant, like wool. This is the best solution for curtain fabric as its drape and natural feel is unaffected.

Secondly, and importantly for upholstery fabric, the material can be treated by applying a fire-retardant back-coating. This stiffens the fabric and makes it better for use as upholstery, but it's not suitable for use in curtains as the drape of the fabric is affected by the fire-retardant coating.

The third method of making upholstery flame retardant is called chemical dipping. This is most often utilised for fabrics made from or containing a high proportion of natural fibres.

Flame resistant (FR)

FR fabric brands are made up of (usually) synthetic fibres that don't catch alight even after being exposed to flame or heat for a long time. Because of their make-up, these fabrics are sometimes referred to as 'inherently flame-retardant fabrics'. Instead of burning, the fabrics eventually start to melt. The amount of permanent flame-resistant fibres found in a flame-resistant fabric can vary widely from a few per cent to 100%, depending on the manufacturer.

GOTS

GOTS is the major fabric processing standard for organic fibres in the industry. This ensures sustainability when it comes to certifying textiles as organic from the moment they're harvested and right through the entire manufacturing process. The fabric is checked throughout the process to ensure there are no chemicals employed in creating it that are harmful to humans or affect animal welfare, and that farmers' working conditions are decent.

GOTS is the most important of the textile exchange certification bodies. It sets the standard for fabric processors, manufacturers and suppliers. Once a fabric has GOTS certification, it's guaranteed organic and can be exported.

This certification is accepted in every major global market. GOTS also gives consumers the assurance that products are sourced from a green supply chain.

Light fastness 1-7

Light fastness is a property of a fabric colourant such as dye or pigment. It describes how resistant the dyed fabric is to fading when exposed to light. Dyes and pigments are applied to colour various materials such as textiles and plastics. They are also employed for manufacturing paints and printing inks.

Colour fading is caused by the molecules in the fabric reacting to ultraviolet light, usually sunlight. If a textile encounters light, the colours can fade or bleach. Materials that don't fade or bleach are said to be lightfast.

To test whether a fabric is lightfast or not, a sample is exposed to a light source for a particular period of time. It is then compared to a sample that has not been exposed to light.

Sustainable fabrics

Not aiming to pick favourites, I just want to share with you the definitions of organic cotton and recycled polyester. There is a lot of noise around these two fabrics. Customers often buy products that use them simply because they sound good. They feel that they are contributing to a larger cause by doing so. Even though that's true, I have found that there are brands that use them even though they don't actually know how they help.

Organic cotton

You might be drawn to the world of the organic while wondering how it is truly sustainable. A lot of farming industries have moved far from the natural product, using all sorts of processes to produce a fruit or vegetable with the perfect shape and colour. They also use chemicals and pesticides and have done for years to prevent crops from being destroyed by disease or insects.

I was walking with my mother in a Greek food market and saw strangely shaped fruit and vegetable items. I picked up one and looked at it. My mother came closer and smiled.

'This is what you call an organic apple,' she said. 'Here, we just call it an apple.'

Cotton has historically been produced using methods that are heavy on chemicals and pesticides. These uncontrolled farming methods also use vast amounts of water. To gain its organic status, cotton must be produced sustainably and ethically.

To grow organic cotton, a farmer has to fertilise the soil in a particular way and use a specific type of seeds. Genetically engineered seeds cannot be used for organic cotton fibre to be produced. This method also employs chemical-free pesticides and an irrigation system that uses less water than historic methods.

Not all farms can produce organic cotton. They have to be specifically sustainable and organic, which means that no harmful chemicals are used in their soil. Organic farmers need to find natural ways to produce the same results as non-organic farmers. A popular method is to introduce insects to control pests instead of using chemicals and pesticides. They also use natural methods to enhance the soil rather than fossil-fuel-based fertilisers.

Because cotton needs so much water, organic farmers have found many ways to gather and use rainwater instead of drinking water for 81% of their cotton.[38] They are saving a massive 91% on irrigation, too. In fact, soils nourished without harmful chemicals don't need as much water as their non-organic counterparts, either.

Another important aspect of the growing of organic cotton is that organisations like GOTS make sure that the conditions for farm workers are tolerable and humane. This means it is ethically sourced and it's environmentally friendly. Buying organic cotton means you are actively preventing global warming.

Climate change is negatively affecting people and the planet. It has caused several temperature rises and extreme weather patterns. Unfortunately, our society and habits are to blame for these situations. Since the nineteenth century, we've used fossil fuels (coal, gas and oil) to modernise our world. Organic cotton production involves emitting 50% less carbon dioxide than standard cotton growing.[39] That's just another reason to shop for this sustainable material.

A number of organisations have created standards to measure whether cotton is organic or not, and whether it has been produced sustainably. These include Fairtrade UK and GOTS, which both operate globally. Their standards rate the ways in which man-ufacturers create the material, the colourants they utilise to dye the cloth, and the supply chains involved in the cotton trade. These methods all have to be carried out sustainably and transparently. The standards then rate the methods accordingly.

OK, you got me: there is always another side to the story. Nothing is perfect in life, and neither is organic cotton production. Organic cotton farms produce less than regular cotton farms from the same amount of land, so need 25% more land to yield the same result. The world doesn't have the space, so farmers may look for other solutions like deforestation, which would cause even more global warming.

Sometimes, producing organic cotton involves natural pesticides. There are chemicals in these that can harm the environment. In fact, some natural pesticides use even more toxic chemicals than the synthetic pesticides and insecticides used in growing conventional cotton.

Recycled polyester

When you take your bins out on a Wednesday (or whichever day the bins are collected in your neighbourhood), look on the side of the bin truck. There is likely to be an image of a plastic bottle with a think bubble that says, 'When I am recycled, I want to be a picnic bench' next to an image of a colourful bench.

These posters have one goal: to make sure that we throw all bottles in the right bin. After all, if we don't do this correctly, an extra bottle will end up in landfill instead of becoming someone's garden furniture. The feeling we get when we see this type of poster is intended to drive us to do good. Seeing results and others taking action motivates us.

It's not only furniture that can be made out of recycled plastic; polyester fabric can also be produced. This type of fabric is used daily by many brands and manufacturers are sourcing it more and more, but what exactly is it made from?

Recycled polyester (rPET) is an eco-friendly type of cloth. It is a great sustainable choice compared to virgin polyester because the reprocessed textile is produced using renewable raw materials. rPET is created from household items that have been discarded after use, like plastic bottles, straws and containers. It is also made from similar types of plastic waste used by manufacturers and factories, which are melted down and transformed.

The most common method used for this textile is mechanical recycling. This involves melting down the waste items to make new thread, but after it's been recycled this way a few times, the fibre tends to weaken. This is why another form of recycling was created.

The chemical recycling process is more expensive but has longer-lasting effects than mechanical recycling. The fabric is chemically created by dissecting plastic molecules, and then building them up again into yarn. This method of processing maintains the quality of the thread; in fact, the textile can be reprocessed over and over again.

Benefits of using rPET in your business:

- This type of polyester is more sustainable and affordable than virgin polyester.

- It's a durable, long-lasting material for fashion brands.

- The textile is soft, lightweight and gentle on the skin, so it's a popular choice for infants' and children's clothing.

- Swimsuits are often made from this textile as it's resistant to ultraviolet rays.

- For industrial use, these fabrics are an excellent choice. They are long-lasting and can be resistant to fire and insects.

- Plastic pollution is a major environmental issue, so this particular textile offers non-toxic products a second life. This means that the product doesn't end up in the ocean or a landfill. Also, the production process uses 95% less energy than traditional textile printing.

- One of my favourite benefits: printing on these recycled textiles requires a water-free heat transfer process, which is eco-friendly.

Sustainable packaging

Once your product is perfected, you have to decide how it is delivered – the packaging, the courier, the tape can all have an impact on the environment. You don't have to go fully sustainable, so I'm not about to criticise anyone who uses non-sustainable tapes, for example, I just want to spark some thought into what options you have.

The truth is that recycled material still holds a high price tag as the technology evolves, especially when it comes to plastic bags. Through my own research, I have found that a small plastic bag for £0.10 per item would cost £1.00 for the equivalent biodegradable option. At ten times the price, the numbers didn't add up and my business was not able to choose the sustainable option, but this idea has been shelved and will be revisited every three months until we find a supplier with a product and price that meets our needs. Whilst not biodegradable, we ensure all our packaging is from recycled stock where possible, widely recyclable and used sparingly. Training your staff to use packaging efficiently can be an effective way of doing your part to reduce waste.

The market is evolving daily and, thanks to technology, recycled and sustainable products are becoming more affordable. It is up to you to keep an eye on the market and ask your team to be aware of any changes and opportunities. If you are not comfortable with what you find originally, follow my system and revisit new options every three months until you find a good sustainable match for your packaging.

An effective way to stay on top of this is to join like-minded communities. You can find groups on LinkedIn, Facebook and YouTube where you can share your ideas, beliefs and worries. These communities act together, united towards a common goal.

How your business can take action

Along with other businesses in the textile and clothing industry, the team at maake believes in sustainability and working towards improving processes and reducing waste for our factory. We like to partner with others to increase the impact of sustainability.

Let me share a few steps the maake brand has taken as a sustainable printer and manufacturer. This will guide you on what to look for in digital printing textile suppliers.

- **Use pigment or dye sublimation ink methods**. These water-based ink methods are more sustainable than other digital printing techniques. They use 95% less energy than traditional textile printing.

- **Use 100% renewable energy sources**. This is a quick fix for any business and the cost is reasonable.

- **Aim for zero waste.** Don't waste a single fabric. Send any excess textiles and cut-off fabrics to local charities, schools, and other educational institutions so that the material can be reused.

- **Recycle paper and ink waste**. Ensure that the waste won't end up in landfill every year.

- **Reduce the amount of electricity you use**. Special cut-off switches on your machines or computers/lighting save on electricity consumption.

- **Only print on-demand**. Print exactly what your customers order. maake does this and produces no extra waste fabric.

- **Don't use water in processes**. maake uses printing processes for these textiles that produce less than a thimbleful of ink waste per 100 m printed and zero water is used in our printing processes – meaning no effluent and low energy usage.

- **Use sustainable non-toxic inks**. All inks used by maake meet Oeko-Tex and GOTS requirements. These inks are also safe for kids as they are EN71–3 certified.

- **Use 'safe' material**. maake works with ethically sourced material bought from trusted local mills wherever possible. This not only helps the local economy, it also reduces our carbon footprint. In addition, we only work with mills that are REACH-accredited. In fact, many of the mills we work with also hold SEDEX accreditation (certification to ensure supply chain sustainability through environmental, social and governance outcomes).

These are some examples of improvements we have worked on at maake and we continue to search for more daily. Hopefully, this list will spark ideas on how you can improve your premises and processes. At the very least, it will give you an idea of what to look for in suppliers.

Once you are happy with your improvements towards sustainability, you can incorporate information about them into your marketing and messaging. This will help your customers identify themselves – they'll be people with similar visions and passions around sustainability.

Do your customers care?

The short answer is absolutely yes! You have done a lot of work on your messaging and have searched for the ideal customer who aligns with your business values. They appreciate your vision and your mission. They might not be as passionate as you or they might be even more so, but the bottom line is that customers are becoming a lot more conscious of sustainability matters and this influences their buying habits.

From experience, I know a customer will search five businesses on average before they make a purchase decision. They will spend numerous hours on the website of the company they choose, reading content, understanding the brand. In the case of more successful brands, they will follow the owner, the expert who represents it.

This is you. The person who has poured your heart out to build the business and has the vision to achieve greatness. You are the leader, the one who captures the spotlight and shines it on what matters, which is not just the problem you solve for your customer. Just as important is how you solve it, which path you take.

When your customer sees you on social media, in webinars and blogs advocating your values, your vision and explaining how and why you do things a certain way, you will capture their attention for a lifetime. They will buy from you again and again because you don't just solve their problem, you respond to their pain and fix it.

That's why they buy your product. You show them that by doing so, they support a greater cause and a future they want to be part of.

How to give back

Great causes take time and money, and time is often a big barrier for entrepreneurs. Masami Sato, author of *Giving Business*,[40] is an extraordinary woman who directs a lot of energy towards the greater good. She has devoted her career to creating an easy way for business owners to give back to the world and ensure that they can share that with their clients.

Masami co-founded B1G1 with Paul Dunn in 2007 with a simple idea: 'What if every business could make a difference in their own way, just by doing what they normally do?' From there, the business has become a global movement, which maake proudly advocates.

The beauty of B1G1 is that it takes little to no time to become a business for good. The way it is designed is you join as a member and choose the amount you want to donate and the causes you want to donate to. You decide how you want to measure the amount you donate within your company and how often. It could be you take 10p from each item sold or it could be an amount you set per week/month/every time your team achieves a certain goal. There is absolute freedom of choice and no long-term commitment of any sort. What you get out of it is the knowledge that your business is giving back, even if it is the smallest amount.

You can keep it to yourself or you can use B1G1 tools, such as the impact widgets, to share your support with the world. The widgets show the impact you've had, the location you've had it in, the money you've donated if you choose, or you can just use colour intensities. When your customers look at your website and see that you care for more than just profit, they will likely want to know more about your brand, your leadership and your product. It could be the deciding factor for them between buying from your business or choosing a competitor.

ACTION STEPS

In this chapter, we have looked at the topic of sustainability. This is hugely important for all of us to consider; if we don't start looking after our planet right now, the future will be bleak for our children and grandchildren.

Actions you and your brand can take include:

- Familiarising yourself with textile certification.
- Considering using sustainable fabrics in your production.
- Reviewing your packaging and trying to change at least one item to a more sustainable option.
- Reviewing maake's steps and considering the possibilities for your own company.
- Becoming a member of B1G1 and giving back as little or as much as you wish.

Conclusion

Congratulations on reading this book and taking steps to improve what you have already built. I hope the ideas and tools have been valuable, thought-provoking, and inspiring to you. Most of all, I hope you have started to take action.

A lot was covered as we journeyed through the six-step STORMS method. Don't be tempted to put the book on your library shelf and simply say, 'There were some great ideas in there.' If you haven't started already, act right now. Don't save it for tomorrow or the day after. Get your calendar out and plan ahead; work out when and how you'll implement all the things that are missing or need optimising in your business. Some concepts and techniques might be clear to you and some might take time to develop in your mind. Either way, seize the moment and make it happen.

I have taken years to learn how to navigate the tools and best practices in this book, developing the STORMS method by experimenting and spending time and money. I learned through success and failure so that you don't have to. You can choose to take the methodology yourself and use it to optimise your business and your time, and I truly hope you succeed, or you can get support and get results faster.

Either way, with the STORMS method, you can ensure your business has sustainable growth while you have a rewarding personal life and claim your design time back. Your employees will believe in your brand's vision and your marketing will open doors. You can get all of that and more by using the techniques and putting the tools in this book into practice. Follow the steps and make sure you complete them one by one. Then go back and optimise them.

Here's a quick recap of the steps of the STORMS method:

- Systems
- Team
- Operations
- Reaction
- Marketing
- Sustainability

When you are confident that you have covered each one of the steps, you are ready to optimise your business. You are in a position to grow your revenue and enjoy your design time. You can book that holiday you've always wanted, happy in the knowledge that your business will continue to be stable and grow until you return.

Ultimately, your reaction to all you have read will be the point at which your brand pivots. You are in control of your team, your brand, and your revenue. Do not settle for less than what you want from your business.

If you're thinking that this is all great, but you're not sure you can take it on, you're overwhelmed and you need accountability and support, don't hold back; go out there and get that support. Find someone who understands what you need and the specific issues you are facing; this can have a great impact on you and your business. Small changes can lead to big results. Is that not something worth looking into?

You have come this far, so allow yourself to feel the success and passion that your work gives you. Don't ever settle for a business that makes you unhappy. You started your brand to capture your dream – now it is time to realise it.

All the best on growing your business sustainably and claiming your design time back,

References

1 Stevenson, A, (Editor) *Oxford Dictionary of English* (Third edition) (Oxford University Press, 2010)

2 Spurgeon, CH, *All of Grace: An earnest word with those who are seeking salvation by the Lord Jesus Christ* (Ichthus Publications, 2014; originally published 1886)

3 Carnegie, D, *How To Win Friends and Influence People* (Vermilion, 2006; first published by Simon & Schuster, 1936)

4 Gerber, ME, *The E-Myth: Why most businesses don't work and what to do about it* (Ballinger, 1998)

5 Evans, R, *The Kid Stays in the Picture* (Hachette Books, 1994)

6 Jager, RD and Ortiz, R, *In The Company of Giants: Candid conversations with the visionaries of the digital world* (McGraw-Hill, 1998)

7 Novais, C, 'When it comes to leadership Alan Mulally will always be the boss' (The Art Of, 2020), www.theartof.com/articles/when-it-comes-to-leadership-alan-mulally, accessed 20 December 2022

8 Erikson, T, *Surrounded by Idiots: The four types of human behaviour (or, How to understand those who cannot be understood)* (Vermilion, 2019)

9 Kvavadze, E, Bar-Yosef, O, Belfer-Cohen, A, Boaretto, E, Jakeli, N, Matskevich, Z, Meshveliani, T, '30,000 years old wild flax fibers – testimony for fabricating prehistoric linen' (*Science*, 24 June 2010), http://nrs.harvard.edu/urn-3:HUL.InstRepos:4270521, accessed 31 January 2023

10 Mount, B, 'The History of Textile Dyes' [blog post] (Faribault Mill, 9 September 2022), www.faribaultmill.com/blogs/the-thread/the-history-of-textile-dyes, accessed 16 December 2022

11 Textile Exchange Team, 'Preferred Fiber & Materials Market Report 2021' (Textile Exchange, 2021), https://textileexchange.org/app/uploads/2021/08/Textile-Exchange_Preferred-Fiber-and-Materials-Market-Report_2021.pdf, accessed 26 January 2023

12 Fischer, G, 'Benjamin Franklin: Advice to a young tradesman' (*The American Instructor* or *Young Man's Best Companion*, 1748) (Founders Online) https://founders.archives.gov/

documents/Franklin/01-03-02-0130, accessed
26 January 2023

13 McCready, A, 'Positive parenting solutions' (no
date), www.positiveparentingsolutions.com/
press, accessed 26 January 2023

14 US Bureau of Labor Statistics, 'Table 5. Number
of private sector establishments by age', www.
bls.gov/bdm/us_age_naics_00_table5.txt,
accessed 26 January 2023

15 Carroll, L, *Alice's Adventures in Wonderland*
(MacMillan, 1865)

16 Gorski, TT, *Getting Love Right: Learning the choices
of health intimacy* (Touchstone, 1993)

17 Dweck, C, *Mindset: The new psychology of success*
(Ballantine, 2007)

18 Mueller, CM, Dweck, CS, 'Praise for intelligence
can undermine children's motivation and
performance' (*Journal of Personality and Social
Psychology*, 1998), https://doi.org/10.1037/0022-
3514.75.1.33, accessed 31 January 2023

19 Scorsese, M (Director); Winter, T (Screenplay),
The Wolf of Wall Street (Paramount Pictures, 2013)

20 Holmes, C, 'The essential guide to marketing
strategy' (Hurree, 2022), https://info.hurree.co/
en/marketing-strategy-essential-guide, accessed
20 December 2022

21 '120+ marketing automation statistics & facts
(2022/2023 Edition)' [blog post] (MarketSplash,
18 January 2023), https://marketsplash.com/
marketing-automation-statistics, accessed
24 January 2023

22 Naragon, K, 'We still love email, but we're spreading the love with other channels' (Business Adobe, 21 August 2018), https://business.adobe.com/blog/perspectives/love-email-but-spreading-the-love-other-channels, accessed 20 December 2022

23 Canada, E, 'Her collaboration with Nespresso' (*Elle*, 20 May 2021), www.ellecanada.com/culture/food-and-drink/an-exclusive-qa-with-the-blond-salads-chiara-ferragni-on-her-collaboration-with-nespresso, accessed 26 January 2023

24 United Nations, 'The Sustainable Development Agenda' (Sustainable Development Goals, 2016), www.un.org/sustainabledevelopment/development-agenda-retired, accessed 20 December 2022

25 Eurostat, 'Generation of waste by waste category, hazardousness and NACE Rev. 2 activity' (Data last updated January 13 2023), https://ec.europa.eu/eurostat/databrowser/view/env_wasgen/default/table?lang=en, accessed 26 January 2023

26 Moore, D, 'UK named fourth largest textile waste producer in Europe' (Circular, 22 January 2020), www.circularonline.co.uk/news/uk-named-fourth-largest-textile-waste-producer-in-europe, accessed November 2022

27 Wrap report, 'Valuing our clothes: The cost of UK Fashion' (Download, September 2020), https://wrap.org.uk/sites/default/files/2020-10/WRAP-valuing-our-clothes-

the-cost-of-uk-fashion_WRAP.pdf, accessed November 2022

28 Sustainable Clothing Action Plan (SCAP 2020), https://wrap.org.uk/taking-action/textiles/initiatives/scap-2020, accessed 20 December 2022

29 Remy, N, Speelman, E and Swartz, S, 'Style that's sustainable: A new fast-fashion formula' (McKinsey Sustainability, 20 October 2016), www.mckinsey.com/capabilities/sustainability/our-insights/style-thats-sustainable-a-new-fast-fashion-formula, accessed 20 December 2022

30 Thomas, D, 'The high price of fast fashion' (*The Wall Street Journal*, 29 August 2019), www.wsj.com/articles/the-high-price-of-fast-fashion-11567096637, accessed 26 January 2023

31 Clarke, R, 'Fast fashion's carbon footprint' (Carbon Literacy Project, August 2021), https://carbonliteracy.com/fast-fashions-carbon-footprint, accessed 20 December 2022

32 UNEP, 'Emissions gap report 2022' (UN Environment Programme, 27 October 2022), www.unep.org/resources/emissions-gap-report-2022, accessed 25 November 2022

33 ILO, 'The Rana Plaza accident and its aftermath' (International Labour Organization, 2022), www.ilo.org/global/topics/geip/WCMS_614394/lang--en/index.htm, accessed 20 December 2022

34 Guardian Staff, 'Bangladesh factory collapse: pope condemns "slave labour" conditions' (*The Guardian*, 1 May 2013), www.theguardian.com/world/2013/may/01/bangladesh-factory-pope-slave-labour, accessed 25 November 2022

35 Dinesh, G, Raghunathan, R and Wang, W, 'Research: When consumers feel less powerful, they seek more variety, (*Harvard Business Review*, 19 October 2022), https://hbr.org/2022/10/research-when-consumers-feel-less-powerful-they-seek-more-variety, accessed 30 October 2022

36 'The key to confidence: What does it take to build trust with busy, sustainability-minded consumers?' (Oeko-Tex, 5 March 2018), www.oeko-tex.com/en/news/press-releases/the-key-to-confidence-what-does-it-take-to-build-trust-with-busy-sustainability-minded-consumers, accessed 20 December 2022

37 Textile Exchange Team, 'Textile Sustainability Conference 2021 Overview Report' (Textile Exchange, 2021), https://textileexchange.org/app/uploads/2021/12/2021-Conference-Overview-Report.pdf, accessed August 2022

38 Organic Cotton Plus Team, 'Organic cotton 101: What is organic cotton?' (Organic Cotton Plus, no date), https://organiccottonplus.com/pages/learning-center, accessed 16 May 2022

39 Fibre2Fashion, 'Organic cotton production emits 50% less C02' (Fashion Network, 11 March 2016), https://in.fashionnetwork.com/news/-organic-cotton-production-emits-50-less-co2-,668194.html, accessed 26 January 2023

40 Sato, M, 'Giving Business: Creating maximum impact in a meaning-driven world' (Buy1Give1, 10 May 2016)

Acknowledgements

In business and in life, ideas come to us from many sources. They come from people we meet for the first time and others who have been our mentors or friends for years.

Reading articles and following the works of leaders and top entrepreneurs has inspired me and given me a path towards something great. I would like to take a moment to thank these people publicly from the bottom of my heart. They might not know it, but they are a big part of my journey.

My biggest thank you goes to my incredible husband, Alexander. In business and in life, you are always by my side, and you don't shy away from hard work. You are patient and so incredibly kind. You have been supportive in all that I want to achieve, and you make sure that the family gets the time together it deserves.

To my gorgeous boys who are the light of my life, thank you for being so kind and wonderful. Aristotelis, your inquisitive nature and your endless questions about business and marketing are impressive. You are so little, and yet you comprehend so many concepts; it's a real pleasure to listen to your theories and examples. Apollon, your smile and cuddles give me strength to work even when I am tired, because I know I will get more time with you in the morning. Having you both has helped me develop my method and understanding on dealing with sensitive work situations and staff.

To my family, I can never thank you enough for the sacrifices you have made and the opportunities you have given me in life. Your daily support and your business savvy have been instrumental in my success, endlessly inspiring, making me believe that anything is possible.

To my mother, father and amazing brother, Hermes. Your way with people is your greatest asset and I am lucky to have you by my side. Thank you all for standing by me, always; for helping me out in my first business and asking nothing in return; for being there when I need you. For your advice, support and help in any way you can give it.

To my fearless mother-in-law, Cathy. You have been a big part of my journey; thank you for believing in Alexander and me and for being there every step of the way. Daisy, Daniel, Monika and Robert: you have all helped in your own way, so thank you. Giannis, your understanding of who I am and what I am trying to achieve has been more valuable than you know. Thank you for always asking me the difficult questions and leading me to new perspectives.

To Lucy, Joe, Alison and the team at Rethink Press - thank you for making this book a reality. I am also indebted to my amazing beta readers, Alexander, Antonio, Bijal and Sharon. Your comments, notes, praise and encouragement helped me finalise my script to a high standard. Rachael, it is an honour to have such an accomplished individual in the industry, who helps designers realise their artistic dreams, write the foreword.

I would like to thank Daniel Priestley: you made me believe that the STORMS method had to be seen and read. David Horne, your optimism and advice has been invaluable. Allan Dib – every time I speak with you, you open my mind to bigger things. You motivate me and help me see that everything is possible if I just sit and do it. It's that simple. Your wonderful quotes are much appreciated.

Finally, I would like to thank my team and my clients who have allowed me to be part of their journey, especially the first ones who gave me the chance to achieve what I have today. Thank you all for believing in me and trusting me.

The Author

 A creative entrepreneur, profit guide and adventurous marketer based in London, Artemis Doupa is on a mission to eradicate designer poverty and increase sustainability. She specialises in one-to-one coaching of visionary fashion and interior designers who want to grow their business and have an impact in their market while still doing what they love. Her signature method gives them the tools to do this while building a fast-growing, long-lasting, successful brand.

Artemis is fully knowledgeable in all eight types of digital fabric printing. In the past ten years, she has worked with over 10,000 brands including Dior,

Alexander McQueen and ASOS through her various businesses. Many of Artemis's clients have become industry leaders with seven-figure revenues and raving fan bases.

Artemis's masters' degree in Architecture and years dedicated to teaching in the UK's most prestigious universities have given her a great sensibility and a common language with all designers. After working in and running a number of successful businesses, in 2016, she co-founded one of the UK's leading digital textile printing companies, maake. Her passion for entrepreneurship couldn't be contained and soon after she founded maakeacademy and maakehome. Artemis's determination to create awareness and be part of a more sustainable future led her to launch an innovative initiative, maakeLess fabric waste, which brings together industry leaders and concerned designers to collaborate on giving fabric a second life.

Find Artemis online at:

🌐 www.artemisdoupa.com

🌐 www.maakeacademy.com

◎ www.instagram.com/artemisdoupa

in www.linkedin.com/in/artemisdoupa

You can also email her at artemis@maakeacademy.com. She responds personally to all emails.